Jimi Hendrix

"Kiss The Sky"

Edward Willett

 Enslow Publishers, Inc.
40 Industrial Road
Box 398
Berkeley Heights, NJ 07922
USA

http://www.enslow.com

Library of Congress Cataloging-in-Publication Data

Willett, Edward, 1959–
    Jimi Hendrix : "Kiss the sky" / by Edward Willett.— 1st ed.
        p. cm. — (American rebels)
    Includes bibliographical references and index.
    ISBN-10: 0-7660-2449-0
    1. Hendrix, Jimi—Juvenile literature. 2. African American guitarists—Biography—Juvenile literature. 3. Rock musicians—United States—Biography—Juvenile literature. I. Title: Kiss the sky. II. Title. III. Series.
    ML410.H476W53 2006
    787.87'166092—dc22

                                            2005033751
ISBN-13: 978-0-7660-2449-6

Printed in the United States of America

10 9 8 7 6 5 4 3 2

Photos and Illustrations: All interior photos courtesy of Everett Collection, Inc.; except p. 43, courtesy of ShutterStock, Inc.

Cover Illustration: Everett Collection, Inc.

Contents

Chapter 1

Guitar God

Shortly after 9:00 A.M. on Saturday, September 24, 1966, a young man stepped off a Pan American Airlines airplane at London's Heathrow Airport. All he had with him was $40 in borrowed cash, a small bag containing a change of clothes, pink plastic hair curlers, a jar of Valderma face cream . . . and his guitar.[1]

That guitar was all he really needed. Within an extraordinarily short time, that young man would be famous around the world. Decades later, he is still famous: "King Jimi," a "guitar god," the "master of electric-guitar sound and style."[2]

Later that same evening, Jimi Hendrix was onstage at The Scotch of St. James, a club that attracted people in the music industry. As he started to play, the club fell silent.

"He was just amazing," Kathy Etchingham, then

just twenty-four and soon to be Jimi's girlfriend (one of many), recalled. "People had never seen anything like it."[3]

Among the musicians in the crowd was Eric Burdon of the Animals. His take: "It was haunting how good he was. You just stopped and watched."[4]

Burdon was the first famous guitarist to be awed by Hendrix's ability. He would not be the last. On January 11, 1967, Hendrix and his new band, The Experience, played at a basement club called the Bag O'Nails in the Soho district of London.

Hendrix had been in England just three-and-a-half months (and had spent several weeks touring France and Germany with The Experience). That night his show was attended by rock greats Pete Townshend and John Entwhistle of the Who; John Lennon, Paul McCartney, and Ringo Starr of the Beatles (plus their manager, Brian Epstein); Mick Jagger and Brian Jones of The Rolling Stones; Eric Clapton, Jimmy Page, Jeff Beck . . . and many others.[5]

People all over the world stopped and watched when Jimi Hendrix played—but it all ended on September 18, 1970, when he died in London at the age of twenty-seven.

Jimi Hendrix crammed a lot into his short life. The consummate rebel, he somehow fought his way past every barrier between him and his lifelong dream of stardom. He rebelled against his father, who thought his music was a waste of time. He rebelled against the strict regimentation of the bands in which he played as a back-up guitarist. He rebelled against the expectation that he would limit himself to playing for African-American audiences. He rebelled against conventional notions of how the electric guitar should be played. He rebelled against conventional ideas of sexual morality. And, tragically and fatally, he rebelled against restrictions on his use of drugs.

Tony Palmer, a friend of Hendrix's and a renowned director of music documentaries, wrote in *The Observer* newspaper on September 20, 1970, "Whatever Mozart and Tchaikovsky have come to mean to lovers of classical music, Hendrix meant the same if not more to a whole generation."[6] He added, "Jimi Hendrix was born Jimi Hendrix. Great musicians are not created; they are *born*. Jimi was meant for music."[7]

Looking back, it seems as if Jimi Hendrix was always meant to be a star. Certainly *he* always thought so. But for most of his life, stardom seemed very far away.

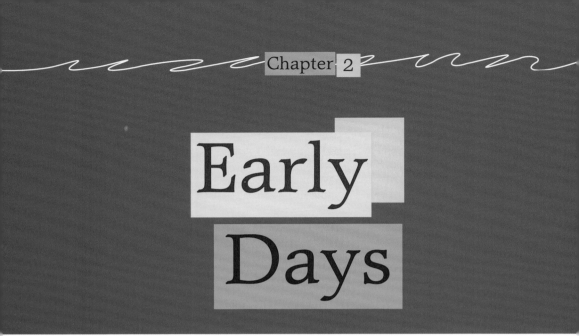

Chapter 2

Early Days

On November 26, 1942, at around 5:00 P.M., a seventeen-year-old girl was admitted to King County Hospital in Seattle. The next morning at 10:15 A.M. she gave birth to an eight-pound boy with lots of hair and big eyes.[1]

The girl was Lucille (Jeter) Hendrix, and the child, whom she named Johnny Allen Hendrix, would later become James Marshall Hendrix, and eventually, Jimi Hendrix.

Lucille Jeter had been just sixteen years old—and already pregnant—when she married Al Hendrix, Jimi's father. Lucille was the last of eight children born to Preston and Clarice Jeter. Clarice, born in Little Rock, Arkansas, in 1894, counted both slaves and Cherokees among her ancestors. Preston Jeter was nineteen years older. The son of a former slave, he was born in Richmond, Virginia, on July 14, 1875. As a young man, Preston witnessed a lynching and decided to leave the

South for the Northwest, where he met and married Clarice.

Clarice's sisters had brought her to Seattle in search of a husband because she was pregnant as the result of a rape. They placed a newspaper ad, which Preston answered. He finally agreed to marry her after the child was born and put up for adoption. By way of a reward, Clarice's sisters gave him a sizeable dowry.

Clarice worked as a domestic servant, while Preston worked as a longshoreman. Of their eight children, two died in infancy and two were given up for adoption. When Lucille was born on October 12, 1925, she was at first raised by her sisters, Nancy, Gertrude, and Delores, because of her parents' poor health. Later the children were fostered for a time with a big German farm family north of Greenlake, Washington.

Lucille grew up pretty, tiny, and pale-skinned. She was not allowed to go to dances until she was fifteen, but then she made up for lost time. In November 1941, Lucille, just turned sixteen and still in junior high school, stopped by the home of a classmate on her way to one such dance. The classmate had a visitor, a young man from Canada named Al Hendrix.[2]

The Dancer from Vancouver

James Allen (Al) Hendrix, Jimi's father, was born on June 10, 1919, in Vancouver, British Columbia. His father, Bertran Philander Ross Hendrix, born in Urbana, Ohio, in 1866, had been a special constable in Chicago and a stagehand in a vaudeville troupe. While touring with the troupe he met and married a dancer named Nora Rose Moore. Unhappy with conditions for blacks in the United States, he took her north to Canada in 1912. Al was their fourth child, following Leon, Patricia, and Frank.

Al remembered his early years fondly. "We were always together and I was well taken care of," he said. But in 1932 his oldest brother, Leon, died of peritonitis brought on by a ruptured appendix. Two years later Al's father died. The family broke up: Pat and Frank got married and Al, just fifteen years old, had to fend for himself.

Al stood only a little over five feet tall, but he tried boxing and did well enough to make it to the finals of the big Golden Gloves tournament in Seattle in 1936. But, he said, "I didn't have the killer instinct."

Dancing was another matter. Al loved dancing. He began performing with a white band in Vancouver and doing guest spots with touring vaudeville shows that came to town. But he could not make a living as a dancer, and he could not find any other jobs; he was too small to work for the railroads, who offered the best jobs available for black people in Vancouver.[3]

And so he headed back to Seattle. On the night he met Lucille Jeter, he accompanied her to Washington Hall, where the great jazz pianist Fats Waller was performing. Lucille, he discovered, enjoyed dancing as much as he did—and could match his skill. They began dating, and eventually formally courting, with Al regularly visiting her parents.

On December 7, 1941, the Japanese attacked Pearl Harbor, plunging the United States into the Second World War. Late in the winter of 1942, Al Hendrix, twenty-two, received his draft notice. The same week, Lucille found out she was pregnant.[4]

Al told Preston Jeter he would marry Lucille, but Preston, furious, tried to talk his daughter out of any such marriage. He failed: Al Hendrix and Lucille Jeter were married on March 31, 1942, at the King County Courthouse.[5] Three days later, Al was shipped out to basic training in Oklahoma.[6]

Buster and Lucille

Lucille hid her pregnancy and her marriage from her junior high-school classmates for a while but soon dropped out. She worked as a waitress (and sometimes singer) in night clubs, lying about her age. She quit work when her pregnancy began to show late that summer. She was living with a family friend, Dorothy Harding, when the baby was born.

Lucille's sister Delores nicknamed the little boy Buster, after Buster Brown, a comic-strip character (as well as the name of a line of children's shoes). To the people that knew him as a child, Jimi Hendrix would be "Buster" for the rest of his life.[7]

Al Hendrix's army career took him from Oklahoma to Georgia to Alabama. Army regulations required that he be given furlough to attend the birth of his son, but his commanding officer, convinced he would go AWOL (Away Without Leave), instead locked him in the stockade, where he received a telegram telling him about Jimi's birth.[8] Before long Al was shipped out to the South Pacific. He would not see "Buster" for three years.

"Lucille didn't even know how to change a diaper at first," Dorothy Harding remembered. Lucille also did not have a place of her own, and nobody really had room for her and Jimi. She moved from Dorothy Harding's to the home of Lucille's sister Delores and back again.

In June of 1943, Lucille's father died. Lucille continued to work in restaurants and taverns while Dorothy, Delores, or her mother Clarice watched Jimi. With Al still far away, Lucille found other men to keep her company. One, John Page, took her and Jimi to Portland, Oregon, where Lucille's relatives found her in a hospital: She had been beaten. Page was arrested, charged with transporting a minor over state lines (Lucille was still only seventeen), and sentenced to five years in prison.

When Jimi was about two-and-a-half, Clarice and Lucille took him to Berkeley, California, for a convention of the Pentecostal Church. A friend of Clarice's named Mrs. Champ liked little Jimi, and when Lucille returned to work in Seattle and Clarice headed to Missouri to visit relatives, Mrs. Champ took his care temporarily. "Temporarily" stretched into weeks, then months. It looked like Jimi might have found a permanent home.[9]

Mrs. Champ's bungalow, a few blocks from the University of California, was the finest house Jimi had ever lived in. He loved being read to, and his vocabulary blossomed. "They called me a little chatterbox," he said.

Back to Seattle

But late in 1945, Al Hendrix was released from the army. A few weeks later he went to Berkeley. After staying a few days to let Jimi get used to him, he packed up the boy's belongings and took him back to Seattle by train. "I just bawled," Jimi recalled. He had begun to feel that Mrs. Champ and her children (a grown daughter and two teenagers) were his family. "I knew they loved me, that they would miss me. . . . That time has always been like a cozy little dream in my mind."[10]

Al Hendrix was debating divorcing Lucille, primarily because he knew she had become involved with a man named John Williams. He ultimately decided against divorce because of "the $25 I had to pay the attorney."[11] But he legally changed Johnny Allen Hendrix's name to James Marshall Hendrix, because it bothered him that his son might be named after another man. From then on, "Buster" was also known as "Jimmy."[12]

Shortly after Al and Jimi returned from California, Lucille joined them, and for a few months they all lived as a family with Delores. Al and Lucille "had their honeymoon then," Delores said. They would go to nightclubs, and she would look after Jimi; then during the day they would look after her children while she worked.[13]

Jimi Hendrix with his father, Al. When he was three years old, Jimi had his name legally changed by his father from "Johnny Allen" to "James Marshall."

But Delores did not like Al and Lucille's drinking, and so when Al found work at a slaughterhouse, the family moved to a hotel room. Then Al received his merchant's marine license and got work on a ship heading to Japan.

When Al returned weeks later, he discovered Lucille had been evicted. He claimed it was because she had been caught in the room with another man, but he and Lucille got back together just the same. For years, their relationship followed that on-again, off-again pattern. "My mother and father used to fall out a lot," Jimi later said. "I always had to be ready to go tippy-toeing off to Canada."[14]

Jimi came to look forward to those trips. In Vancouver, he would stay with Grandma Nora, the ex-vaudeville dancer. "Gramma would tell me little Indian stories that had been told to her when she was my age; I couldn't wait to hear a new story," he said. "She had Cherokee blood. So did Gramma Jeter. I was proud that it was in me, too."

In Seattle, his grandmother Clarice would take him to the Pentecostal Church of God in Christ, where he learned hymns he could still hum as an adult. She also took him to movies, which he loved his whole life.[15]

But at home in the Rainier Vista Housing Project, which at least now was a proper house, things were difficult. A lot of the time his mother was not around. When she was, she and Al would drink, and when they drank, they fought. Delores and Dorothy noticed that

Jimi became very quiet that year, and when they asked him why, he would cite his parents' constant fighting as the cause.

The Family Expands

On January 13, 1948, Al and Lucille had a second son, Leon. Dorothy Harding recalled how happy Al was to see the baby born, because he had missed Jimi's birth.

Things were pretty good for a while after Leon's birth. The family moved into a larger two-bedroom unit. That fall, Jimi started kindergarten. But just eleven months after Leon was born, Lucille had a third son, Joseph, who suffered from various birth defects. His need for medical care became one more thing to fight over. Lucille blamed Joseph's problems on Al pushing her while she was pregnant; he blamed them on Lucille's drinking. (Much later, Al claimed he was not really Joseph's father, a claim eventually born out in court.) Lucille found out that the state would pay for the majority of Joseph's medical needs, but the family would have to pay for some. Al, then working as a night janitor, refused to pay for any of it.

The family barely scraped by. Leon and Jimi might have suffered serious malnutrition if neighbors had not fed them almost every day, so Al decided to send all three boys north to Vancouver. Jimi started first grade there, but in October the boys returned to Seattle, where Al and Lucille were together again . . . for the moment.

By the fall of 1950, the family situation had deteriorated, and Jimi was living with Delores. He started second grade at Horace Mann Elementary. On September 27, the Hendrix's fourth child, Kathy Ira, was born sixteen weeks premature and blind. At the age of eleven months, she was put into foster care as a ward of the state. (Al later claimed he was not her father, either.)

A year later, Lucille had another daughter, Pamela. (Again, Al claimed he was not the father.) Pamela, too, had health problems and was quickly fostered out.

End of a Marriage

When Pamela was born, Jimi had just started third grade. Not long after his ninth birthday in November, Lucille left Al. They were officially divorced on December 17, 1951, although they would continue an on-and-off relationship.[16] (In fact, Lucille had another son with Al; Alfred Hendrix, born on February 14, 1953. He also had birth defects and was put up for adoption immediately.)[17] Al was given custody of the three boys, but in the summer of 1952, Joseph was made a ward of the state; it was the only way he could get the medical treatment he needed.[18]

Neighbors and relatives actually did most of the raising of Jimi and Leon. And, to a certain extent, Jimi raised his younger brother.

Among the people Jimi occasionally lived with over the next few years were Al's brother Frank and his wife, Pearl, and their two children, Diane and Bob; Grace Hatcher, the daughter of Al's sister Pat, and her husband Frank, who also had children of their own; and Al's friends Ernestine and Bill Benson. "My Dad really just dumped us with people while he was running around drinking, gambling, and showing off to women," Jimi said later. "He always needed lots of attention."[19] Others who looked after the boys included Grandma Clarice Jeter, Grandma Nora Hendrix in Vancouver, Aunt Delores Hall, and Dorothy Harding.[20]

> **To a certain extent, Jimi raised his younger brother.**

Al used to threaten the children that he would send them to their mother's if they misbehaved, but, Leon recalled, "Me and Jimmy used to get into trouble on purpose so we could go visit our mother . . . That was what we wanted!" Sometimes they saw her when they were not supposed to. "We'd walk over to her house . . . we had more fun with her . . . She'd give us all the love she had for a few days, then she'd be gone for a few months."[21]

Jimi in School

Jimi had a good school attendance record at first, but that fell off in later grades. His grades were nothing to brag about. His best subject was not music—it was art.[22]

"Wherever we lived, he was always making pictures," Leon recalled. "He loved those color pencils, and he'd fiddle around trying to choose just the right color."[23] He liked to draw flying saucers, drag racers and other automobiles—he even mailed some automobile designs to the Ford Motor Company.[24]

The brothers' official residence varied with Al's

18

fortunes. In the spring of 1953, Al got a better job and bought a two-bedroom house at 2603 South Washington Street. Not long after, Frank and Grace Hatcher moved in to look after the boys. At the end of April, Jimi was transfered to the most racially integrated school in Seattle, Leschi Elementary. (The 46 students in his sixth grade class picture include nearly equal numbers of African Americans, Caucasians, and Asian Americans.)[25]

At Leschi Jimi met his closest childhood friends, Jimmy Williams, Pernell Alexander, and Terry Johnson. (To avoid confusion, Jimi was nicknamed "Henry" and Jimmy was "Potato Chips."[26]) The boys played together in the streets and parks with Jimi's dog, Prince (named after the 1954 adventure movie *Prince Valiant*, which Al took Jimi and Leon to see).[27]

That was also the year Jimi began showing a real interest in music. He started following the pop charts and listening to the radio every day after school, strumming along on a broom as if it were a guitar. Jimi and Jimmy liked crooners: Frank Sinatra, Nat King Cole, Perry Como, and especially Dean Martin. Al disapproved of Jimi's "air-guitar"; he thought a broom should only be used for sweeping and would get mad when he would discover straw on the floor from Jimi's make-believe playing.[28]

Al, always struggling with drinking and gambling, moved from low-paying job to low-paying job. In 1954 the welfare department began keeping a close watch on the family, and in 1956, when the house Al had bought in 1953 was sold because he could not pay the bills, Leon was fostered out. He would return periodically over the next few years, but whenever Al ran into difficulties, off he would go again. He eventually lived in seven different foster homes, though fortunately close enough that he and Jimi still saw each other almost constantly.

As Al moved from low-rent place to low-rent place, Jimi had to keep changing schools. He started the 1955–56 school year at Meany Junior High, transferred to Washington Junior High in February, and was back at Meany in the fall.[29] He continued to find food and shelter with family and friends as often as with his father.

First Guitar, First Girlfriend

For a while Al and Jimi lived in a rooming house run by a Mrs. McKay. Her paraplegic son played a beat-up acoustic guitar with a single string. Jimi (with help from family friend Ernestine Benson, who lived with the Hendrixes for a while and whose record collection gave Jimi his first exposure to the blues) bought the guitar for five dollars. "He only had one string," Benson said, "but he could really make that string talk." Jimi never let that guitar out of his sight; at night, he held it on his chest.[30]

On September 1, 1957, Elvis Presley performed in Seattle's Sick's Stadium. Jimi watched from a hill overlooking the field. He later said what really impressed him was the backup band. "Man, they were cool! They made playing music seem like the best thing in the world."[31]

Later that school year, Jimi met his first girlfriend, Carmen Goudy, who was thirteen. Too poor to do anything else, they would walk in the park and talk about their dreams. Jimi told Carmen what he wanted most was a real guitar, because he was going to become a famous musician. He had finally gotten strings for his beat-up acoustic, and he strummed it constantly, even though its neck was so warped it would not stay in tune.

Jimi was naturally left-handed, but Al tried to make him play right-handed. "My dad thought everything left-handed was from the devil," Leon remembered. (This was a common superstition among people of Al Hendrix's generation.) Jimi restrung the guitar so he could play it left-handed, but whenever Al showed up he flipped it around and played it right-handed.[32]

"I didn't know a thing about tuning," Jimi said later, "so I went down to the store and ran my fingers across the strings on a guitar they had there. After that I was able to tune my own."[33]

Jimi Loses His Mother

Jimi and Leon had not seen their mother in months when they heard that she had married again. But shortly after the January 3, 1958, wedding to the much older William Mitchell, a retired longshoreman, she ended up in the hospital with hepatitis (probably the result of liver damage brought on by excessive drinking).

The boys' Aunt Delores took them to visit her, and

she hugged and kissed them. After they had left, she told her sister "I'm not going to make it." Despite her dire prediction, she left the hospital the next week, but a few days later, on February 2, she was found unconscious outside a tavern and taken to the hospital, where she died of a ruptured spleen.[34]

A friend came to the boardinghouse where Al and the boys were living and told Al. Jimi overheard the news and burst into tears. Al took the boys to the funeral home but left them in the truck while he went in to view the body. When the funeral was held on February 5 at a Pentecostal church, neither Al nor the boys attended. Al claimed that he could not go because he did not have a car, but the boys could have gone. Leon, however, said that Al refused permission.[35] Jimi "never really forgave our dad," Leon said.[36]

Focused on Music

Always shy and introverted, Jimi became even more so after his mother's death, pouring himself into his music. "Words meant nothing to me then," he said later. At times, he said, he "felt as if I was flying, *soaring*. I felt *free*, like I could do most anything. I played for *me*."[37]

That spring, Jim and Al moved into a two-bedroom house with Cornell and Ernestine Benson (Leon was back in foster care). All the moves, the school changes that went with them, and Jimi's penchant for skipping school (often to visit neighborhood musicians) affected his grades to the point where he was forced to repeat ninth grade in the fall of 1958.

He did not do much better the second time around. In December, he and Al moved again to stay for a few months with Grace and Frank Hatcher, forcing Jimi to change schools yet again. He would not have advanced to high school in the fall of 1959 except for the fact that school officials were only allowed to hold him back for one year.

All Jimi really cared about was playing the guitar. And in the spring of 1959, Al Hendrix (at the urging of Ernestine Benson) made Jimi the happiest boy on earth: he bought him an electric guitar.[38]

Chapter 3

The Music Begins

Jimi had an electric guitar, but he did not have an amplifier. Or a guitar case. Or a band.

Over the next few months, Jimi played with any musician who owned any kind of instrument in the neighborhood. (That briefly included his father, who bought a saxophone at the same time as Jimi's guitar but soon returned it.)

At first, Jimi knew lots of riffs (short, catchy musical phrases) but no songs. But he learned fast, as fast as a song a day; his friend Jimmy Williams called him "a human jukebox." His favorite song that first summer with an electric guitar was Dean Martin's "Memories Are Made of This."[1]

In the fall of 1959, Jimi started tenth grade at Garfield High School, one of the best and most integrated high schools in the city. "Our neighbors were African-Americans, Jewish, Chinese, Russian; therefore that's what the school looked like," recalled Carroll Brown, a classmate of Jimi's. "We were taught to respect one another's cultures."[2]

Jimi had made it to high school by the skin of his teeth, but he showed no inclination to pull up his grades. "He probably could have got straight A's at school, but he wasn't into that," his brother Leon said.[3] Instead, he focused on reconnecting with friends like Jimmy Williams and Pernell Alexander, whom he had missed for a year while he was held back a grade—and trying to get into a band.

Jimi Joins the Velvetones

Jimi Hendrix's first formal gig was with a band made up of older boys who were auditioning him to see if he could be a permanent part of their group. The band played in the basement of the Temple De Hirsch Sinai, a Seattle synagogue. His girlfriend Carmen Goudy was there. "During the first set, Jimi did his thing," she remembered. "He did this wild playing, and when they introduced the band members and the spotlight was on him, he became even wilder."[4] A little too wild, it turned out: the band kicked Jimi out before returning for the second set.

Jimi and Carmen soon drifted apart, as Carmen became interested in other boys who actually had enough money to take her on dates. Jimi began dating Betty Jean Morgan, first asking her father if he could take her out. "He was a sweetheart. My parents liked him because he was polite," Betty Jean remembered.[5]

Soon Jimi finally did join a band, the Velvetones, whose sound mixed jazz, blues, and rhythm and blues

(R&B), and dance. "Each show had dance numbers," tenor sax player Luther Rabb remembered. "We had to dress up and glue glitter on our pants so they'd be shiny." Jimi was not the best guitar player in the band, but he kept improving—and he was always flashy.[6]

The Velvetones landed a steady gig at a club called Birdland, which earned Jimi the right to hear other bands that played there for free. He took to doing 10-minute solo acts while a band led by Dave Lewis was on break. "He would play this wild stuff, but the people couldn't dance to it," Lewis remembered. "They just stared at him."[7]

Al Hendrix, despite having finally bought Jimi a guitar, did not much like his son's musical activities. Anthony Atherton, a member of the Velvetones, said Jimi kept his guitar at Pernell Alexander's house for fear his father would destroy it. "His father was pretty much against it, and music in the house, even practicing. Anyone who came around with an instrument was really in trouble."[8]

A Heartbreaking Loss

And then, one night after the band played at Birdland, Jimi left his guitar backstage. When he went back the next day, it had been stolen. "He was absolutely crushed," recalled Leon. "But I think he was even more upset that he knew he had to tell our dad, and he knew he was going to get a big whipping."[9]

As Al remembered it, "He didn't tell me about it for a long time. He said he left it over at James Thomas's.

I dropped him over there and said to bring his equipment home and that's when he told me he'd got it stolen. So I says, 'You're gonna have to do without a guitar for a while.'"[10]

The theft came just when Jimi had started playing with a better band, the Rocking Kings. Fortunately, he had impressed them enough that some band members pitched in to buy him a new Danelectro Silvertone guitar ($49.95 from Sears Roebuck), complete with matching amplifier.[11] Jimi promptly painted it red, and added the name "Betty Jean" in two-inch-high letters.

Rocking with the Rocking Kings

The Rocking Kings mixed blues, jazz, and rock. "We'd play anything that would keep people dancing," drummer Lester Exkano recalled.[12] They landed several professional engagements, including Seattle's Seafair Festival, and won second place in an amateur all-state "Battle of the Bands."

In June of 1960 Al and Jimi moved to a house not far from Garfield High. Jimi's tenth grade marks were abysmal. He had a B in art, a D in typing, and Fs in drama, world history, and gym. He had withdrawn from language arts, Spanish, and woodshop or he would have failed them, too. He started eleventh grade that fall, but he continued to skip classes. Late in October, he dropped out.

From the Rocking Kings to the Tomcats

The Rocking Kings broke up after the band's car broke down on a trip to a well-paying gig in Vancouver, British

Columbia, and their impromptu show in Bellingham, Washington, got closed down by police. The manager, James Thomas, reformed the group as Thomas and the Tomcats, making himself front man and giving Jimi back-up vocal duty. (Until then, Jimi had seldom sung; he felt his voice was too weak.)

The changes did not bring in any more money, though, and Jimi was desperately short of cash. The most he ever earned with the Tomcats was $20 a month, and he had to buy his own stage clothes and other gear out of that. At eighteen, he remained dependent on his father, who, according to Leon, "literally said that music was 'the devil's business.'"[13]

Al wanted Jimi to help him in the landscaping business, but Jimi hated it, and Al paid him next to nothing. That spring, one of Al's clients saw Al punch Jimi. Jimi said later, "I had to carry stones and cement all day and he pocketed the money . . . I ran away after a blazing row [argument] with my dad. He hit me on the face and I ran away."[14]

Jimi took to stopping by a burger joint where his friend Terry Johnson worked, across from Garfield High, to collect unsold hamburgers at the end of the day. Even though he was begging for food, that spring he asked Betty Jean to marry him. But she was not due to graduate until 1963, and neither she nor her parents took the proposal seriously.

On May 2, 1961, Jimi was arrested for riding in a stolen car and spent a day in the juvenile detention center before Al bailed him out. Four days later he was arrested for riding in another stolen car. After eight more days in the detention center, he was released to await a court hearing and formal sentencing.

Facing a court hearing, Jimi considered joining the army. His friends Terry Johnson and Jimmy Williams had already enlisted; there simply were not many jobs for young black men. The prosecutor liked the idea: at the May 16 hearing, he agreed to a suspended two-year sentence—provided Jimi joined the army.

Into the Army

The next day, Jimi signed up for three years. That night, panicking, "I sat on the bed and had a little talk with myself," he said. "It might have been the first time I was thinking as a man, not as a dumb kid. I made myself a kind of promise—Don't look back. If you do, it will hold you back."[15]

Jimi played his final gig with the Tomcats the night before he left for basic training. Leon and Betty Jean Morgan attended. Afterward, Jimi gave Betty Jean a rhinestone "engagement ring"—and asked her to keep his guitar until he sent for it.

Carmen Goudy, at the concert with a new boyfriend, noticed how much Jimi's playing had improved. He was still flashy, she said, "But he was good. He was *really* good."[16]

Jimi Hendrix began basic training on May 31, 1961, at Fort Ord, California. Military records state that he weighed 155 pounds and was five feet, ten inches tall.

After losing his first guitar, some fellow musicians bought Hendrix a replacement, which he painted red and named "Betty Jean," after his high school girlfriend.

He wrote numerous letters home to his father, sounding homesick. After about two months, he asked Al to collect his guitar from Betty Jean's mother and send it to him. It arrived on July 31.

Five days later, Jimi completed basic training. At the beginning of September, while waiting for his orders to arrive, he got a week-long leave. He went home, where he spent most of the time with Betty Jean and her parents. He still talked of marrying her.

On Halloween, Hendrix learned he had been assigned to be a supply clerk for the 101st Airborne Division in Fort Campbell, Kentucky. Once there, he began rigorous parachute training.[17]

But he also found time to play his guitar. One day while he was playing in a service club, a serviceman named Billy Cox stopped to listen. Cox, an experienced bass player from Pittsburgh, later said Hendrix's playing sounded like a combination of "Beethoven and [legendary blues guitarist] John Lee Hooker."[18]

"You have real talent," Cox told Hendrix.[19] He introduced himself, checked out a bass (the service club had instruments and amps for rent), and the two started jamming. Cox would be a friend and musical colleague for the rest of Hendrix's life.

Hendrix and Cox formed a five-piece band (with a constantly shifting lineup) that played base clubs on weekends. Cox was not much of a singer, so Hendrix became a lead singer for the first time.

Of course, he also continued parachute training,

earning the coveted 101st Screaming Eagle Patch (the design of which he had long admired—one reason he had asked to be assigned to the Airborne) in January of 1962.

By March of 1962, Hendrix's and Cox's band, the Kasuals, was getting gigs as far away as North Carolina. Touring possibilities were coming up. Cox's enlistment was almost over, but Hendrix still had more than two years to go. He did not want to wait that long.

"The Army's really a bad scene," he said later. "They wouldn't let me have anything to do with music. They tell you what you are interested in and you don't have any choice. The Army is more for people who like to be told what to do."[20]

It was also hazardous, not just because he was jumping out of airplanes, but because there seemed to be an increasing chance he would be sent into combat in one of several global trouble spots, including a country called Vietnam.

And so, Jimi Hendrix decided he had to get out.

Out of the Army

In April and May he began to see the base psychiatrist, claiming he was having homosexual fantasies about his bunkmates. At the time, homosexuals were considered unfit for military service and homosexual conduct was grounds for immediate discharge.

After a complete physical on May 14, during which Hendrix claimed he was suffering from dizziness, chest pains, weight loss, insomnia, and more, the doctor,

Captain John Halbert, recommended that Hendrix be discharged due to his "homosexual tendencies."[21]

Thanks to a bonus for unused leave, Hendrix received three or four hundred dollars when he was discharged. But he blew it all in a single night in a Clarksville jazz club, buying people drinks. When he walked out, he only had $16 left—not enough to return to Seattle as he had planned.

Instead he hung around, playing with the Kasuals on weekends, staying with friends or girls he met at clubs, including one named Joyce. After Billy Cox was released from the Army in September, 1962, he, Hendrix, and Joyce all shared an apartment. Hendrix wrote Betty Jean and told her he would not be returning to Seattle. She sent back his engagement ring.[22]

At about the same time, Hendrix and Cox drove to Indianapolis. The gig they thought they had fell through, so instead they entered a "Battle of the Bands" at a bar. They placed second and impressed Alphonso Young, the guitarist for the winning band. Young quit his band and,

Jimi Tells a Different Tale

Jimi Hendrix never publicly revealed exactly how he got out of the army. He always claimed he was discharged because he broke an ankle on his twenty-sixth jump.

"One day, I got my ankle caught in the sky hook just as I was going to jump and I broke it," he said. "I told them I'd hurt my back too. Every time they examined me I groaned, so they finally believed me and I got out."[23]

However, Army medical files make no mention of such a break.

with Hendrix, Cox, and singer Harry Batchelor, formed the King Kasuals. Hendrix played lead guitar and Young played rhythm. (Young could play the guitar with his teeth. Not wanting to be upstaged, Hendrix soon learned how, too.)[24]

The King Kasuals

The King Kasuals moved back to Tennessee, playing twice a week at Nashville's Del Morocco Club and anywhere else that would have them the rest of the week. Hendrix did not have any more money than he had had in Seattle, but he certainly had more girlfriends. No relationship lasted more than a few weeks, however.

He also had his first experience with drugs. Hendrix practiced guitar every minute he could (Cox said he put in twenty-five years of work on his guitar in five years). He began taking amphetamines so he could stay up all night and practice even more. He also began smoking marijuana, when he could afford it.[25]

> **Billy Cox said [Hendrix] put in twenty-five years of work on his guitar in five years.**

Hendrix talked to, and tried to learn from, every guitarist he met. He became friends with Johnny Jones, guitarist for the Imperials. In the fall of 1962, he tried to take on Jones in a guitar showdown at the club where Jones was playing.

He failed miserably. Some listeners actually laughed at his solos, which sounded like copies of B.B. King's.

"He came looking for a shoot-out, but he was the one who got himself shot," Jones said.[26]

By December, Hendrix decided the King Kasuals were not going to make it. He went to Vancouver to stay with his grandmother Nora. He avoided Seattle, though he telephoned his father. "He made me feel like a failure," Hendrix said. "And of course I was. But I didn't plan to stay one."[27]

The Chitlin' Circuit

For a while Hendrix played rhythm with Bobby Taylor and the Vancouvers, one of whose members was Tommy Chong, later famous as half of the comedy duo Cheech and Chong. But after two months, he headed south again.

For the next two years, from 1963 through 1965, Hendrix played with many different groups on the Chitlin' Circuit, a series of African-American clubs—anywhere black musicians played to black audiences. (Chitlin's, or chitterlings, are a staple of Deep South cooking. They are pig intestines, typically served boiled in a well-seasoned broth or deep-fried in flour.)

Chitlin' Circuit musicians had to be entertainers as well as good instrumentalists. "Down there you have to play with your teeth or else you get shot," Hendrix said. "There's a trail of broken teeth all over the stage."[28]

Hendrix's flashiness sometimes got him in trouble. In the middle of one tour, singer Solomon Burke, an influential pioneer of soul music, got tired of Hendrix's wild solos and traded him to Otis Redding for two horn players. Less than a week later, Redding fired him.[29]

New York, New York

In December 1963, a month after he turned twenty-one, Hendrix headed for New York City by bus, carrying his guitar on his back and everything else he owned in a duffel bag and wearing a beige overcoat given to him by a friend. An offer of work had evaporated, and he found himself alone in a city where he did not know a soul.

Finding work proved difficult. Rock 'n' roll was shunned in Harlem: musicians were expected to play R&B, jazz, or blues. And innovation was frowned upon, whereas Hendrix's preferred style of playing was all about innovation.

Shortly after arriving in New York, Hendrix moved in with Lithofayne (Fayne) Pridgeon. They lived first at the Hotel Seifer and later with her mother.

"People would say, 'If you don't get a job, you'll just starve to death,'" Hendrix told an interviewer years later. "But I didn't want to take a job outside music. I tried a few jobs, including car delivery, but I always quit after a week."[30] Only the kindness of others allowed him to stay so devoted to music. After he broke up with Pridgeon, Hendrix lived for a while with Taharqa and Tunde-Ra Aleem, identical twins who started in the music business, went into drug-dealing, then returned to music.

Hendrix took whatever musical jobs he could get. The first record Jimi Hendrix can be heard playing on that broke the Top 40 was the Don Cobay song "Mercy, Mercy." With the Aleems, he even toured in the back-up band for a stripper for a while.[31]

Finally, in March of 1964, he joined a big-time band, the Isley Brothers (best known for their hit "This Old Heart of Mine" a couple of years later; Ronald Isley, one of the original members, is famous today for his alter ego, Mr. Biggs). Hendrix toured with the group that spring and recorded with them that summer. But the strict regulations suffocated him. "We had white mohair suits, patent leather shoes, and patent leather hairdos," he complained in a 1967 interview. "We weren't allowed to go onstage looking casual. If our shoelaces were two different types, we'd get fined five dollars. Oh man, did I get tired of that!"[32]

Hendrix quit the band in Nashville and joined up with singer Gorgeous George Odell for a short tour. He missed the Gorgeous George tour bus in Kansas City and was stranded. He joined another band within a week, and ended up in Atlanta that summer. There he was hired for Little Richard's band, the Upsetters.

Playing for Little Richard

Little Richard, whose career had been launched by the smash hit "Tutti Frutti," has been called the original wild man of rock 'n' roll, but Hendrix found the Upsetters just as stylistically rigid as the Isley Brothers. He was not allowed to improvise, because no one was allowed to upstage Little Richard. (Years later, Hendrix said he was once ordered to take off the satin shirt he had worn instead of the band's uniform because Little Richard declared, "I am the King of Rock and Roll, and I am the only one allowed to be pretty!"[33]

In Los Angeles on New Year's Eve 1964, Hendrix watched the Ike and Tina Turner Revue, a major husband-and-wife soul act that featured nine musicians and three scantily clad female background singers, and soon had a new girlfriend: Rosa Lee Brooks, a singer he met at the concert. (He played for her on a single called "My Diary" that she cut in early March.) When he left Little Richard's band in March, he immediately joined the Ike and Tina Turner band. But once again he was fired because, Ike Turner said, his solos went on too long.

Hendrix then rejoined Little Richard. But they still did not get along, and he left the Upsetters for good in New York. (Little Richard's brother Robert claimed he fired Hendrix; Hendrix said he quit because he was not getting paid on time.)[34]

By the summer of 1965, Hendrix, using the stage name Maurice James, was back in New York trying to get work as a studio musician. He signed (without reading) a two-year agreement to play guitar at Sue Records. He also played on a series of singles for another label.

In October of 1965, Hendrix began playing with the Squires, run by Curtis Knight. Hendrix was the group's front man. The Knights cut a cover of Bob Dylan's "Like a Rolling Stone" that featured Hendrix, called "How Would You Feel." It was produced by Ed Chalpin of

PPX Enterprises Inc., whose specialty was marketing cover versions of U.S. hits overseas. Upon hearing Hendrix play, Chalpin signed him to a recording and producing contract.

Jimi and the Starliters

Hendrix was not making enough money with the Squires, so he went out on tour again, this time with Joey Dee and the Starliters, a successful band which had had a number-one hit called "Peppermint Twist."

The Starliters were the first band with cross-racial appeal that Hendrix had ever played with. That meant they were the first group Hendrix had played with since the military that played to white audiences.

Although Hendrix liked the other members of the band, he still felt stifled having to play the same songs the same way night after night (although he did get one

The Chalpin Contract

Hendrix once again failed to read the contract he was signing. If he had, he would have seen that it required him to "produce and play and/or sing exclusively for PPX Enterprises Inc., for three years" and specified that he would produce a minimum of three sessions a year.

Compensation was set at one percent of the retail price of all records sold (not a bad royalty at the time). All Jimi received up front, however, was $1.

"He was so happy to be an artist in his own right, he would have signed anything," Chalpin claimed later.

Hendrix played on 33 songs for Chalpin over the next eight months, but that contract he signed without thinking twice would cause him trouble for the rest of his life.[35]

solo each performance). He quit the tour and went back to New York.

For the next few months he played with Curtis Knight and the Squires and did some studio work trying to scrape together enough money to keep going. Fayne Pridgeon, his former girlfriend, had married Taharqa Aleem. Hendrix stayed with them for a while, but that obviously was not an ideal situation, so in January of 1966, he moved into a hotel. He was in danger of eviction when he landed a gig with King Curtis and the All-Stars at an important Harlem club called Small's Paradise.

Although just hired to fill in, Hendrix impressed the band so much that he played with them for several months. "In all my years, I've never seen another guitar player pick up the material like that," said drummer Bernard "Pretty" Purdie.[36]

> "I've never seen another guitar player pick up the material like that."
> —Bernard Purdie

Though struggling to survive, Hendrix soon had a new girlfriend, Diana Carpenter, a sixteen-year-old runaway working as a street prostitute. In early May of 1966, when she told Hendrix she was pregnant, he insisted she stop working.

She had been making more money than he was. Without her income, by late spring they were reduced to stealing to survive. Carpenter secretly went back to work. When Hendrix found out, he hit her with a belt. Carpenter was shocked. "It was the only time he was like that," she said.

Their relationship soon fell apart. After one fight, Carpenter went out, picked up a customer who turned out to be an undercover policeman, and was arrested. Given a choice between three years in prison or a bus ticket home to her parents, Carpenter chose to go home. In February of 1967 she gave birth to a daughter, Tamika. She was convinced Hendrix was the father.[37]

Hendrix promptly started seeing another prostitute, Carol Shiroky, his first white girlfriend. She bought him a new guitar. But another woman he met about the same time would have a far greater impact on his life.

"He was Clearly a Star"

Linda Keith, just twenty years old, was British, Jewish, well-off, educated—and the girlfriend of Keith Richards of the Rolling Stones. The Stones were coming to the United States for a tour that summer, and Linda Keith had come over early to check out the New York clubs—including the Cheetah Club, where Hendrix happened to be playing (for the last time, as it turned out) with Curtis Knight and the Squires.

The band did not impress Keith, but Hendrix did. "The way his hands moved up and down on the neck of the guitar was something to watch," she said. "I found myself simply mesmerized by watching him play . . . He was clearly a star, though he was such an odd-looking star, and it was such an odd place, it didn't seem right."[38]

Keith and her friends invited Hendrix over to their

table between sets, stayed for the last set, and then invited him back to an apartment.

In his biography of Jimi Hendrix, *Room Full of Mirrors*, Charles R. Cross says that in the course of the evening, Linda Keith and her companion introduced Hendrix to LSD. One of Linda's friends asked him if he would be interested in taking some "acid." He replied, "No, I don't want any of that, but I'd love to try some of that LSD stuff."[39]

However, Hendrix told UPI reporter Sharon Lawrence, author of *Jimi Hendrix: The Man, The Magic, The Truth*, that it was Las Vegas prostitute and rock groupie Devon Wilson who introduced him to LSD in late 1965.[40]

Whichever is the truth, LSD would influence Hendrix and his music for the rest of his life.

Keith and Hendrix sat up talking all night long, mostly about music and guitars, while listening to Bob Dylan's new album *Blonde on Blonde*. It was the beginning of a friendship that very soon would have a major impact on Hendrix's career.

Two weeks later Hendrix ran into folk musician Richie Havens (himself later to become world-famous) at the Cheetah while playing with another second-rate band. Havens, impressed with Hendrix's playing, urged him go down to Greenwich Village. He gave Hendrix the names of a couple of clubs, including Café Wha?

Jimmy James and the Blue Flames

Hendrix auditioned at Café Wha? and landed a solo gig. A few days later, while shopping in Manny's Music for

LSD

Lsyergic acid diethylamide, a.k.a. LSD or "acid," was discovered by Dr. Albert Hoffman in 1938 while he was researching ergot fungus, which grows on some grains and grasses and can poison humans and animals. A few years later Hoffman accidentally dosed himself with LSD and discovered it was a hallucinogen—a substance that causes hallucinations.

By the 1940s, Sandoz Pharmaceuticals was commercially marketing LSD. Psychiatrists in Saskatchewan, Canada, conducted some of the most extensive medical testing of the drug in the 1950s. They reported that it could be used to cure alcoholism, and they felt it held promise in the treatment of schizophrenia.

It was Dr. Humphrey Osmond, a British psychiatrist working at the Saskatchewan mental hospital in the town of Weyburn, who coined the term "psychedelic," which he defined as "mind manifesting"—that is, the drug affected the mind rather than the body—to describe LSD.

Official distribution of LSD was stopped in August 1965 as recreational use of it became widespread. It was still legal in the United States in 1966; it was not outlawed until 1967.

The word "psychedelic" soon moved beyond its clinical usage to describe other things: wild color schemes and distorted images reminiscent of LSD-generated hallucinations spread through popular culture and were called psychedelic. Eventually, the whole decade became known as the "psychedelic 60s."

guitars (he had had another one stolen), Hendrix met Randy Wolfe, a fifteen-year-old runaway, and invited him to join his band. He also met Jeff "Skunk" Baxter, a bass player (later part of the Doobie Brothers), and invited him join the band, which Hendrix, then using the stage name Jimmy James, christened Jimmy James and the Blue Flames.

The band played covers, but Hendrix put his unique stamp on them, stretching three-minute pop songs into ten-minute epics. He began to use a crude fuzz box (which produces a distorted, synthetic sound), and incorporate feedback (high-pitched squealing caused by an amplifier picking up and re-amplifying its own sounds). "It was amazing," Danny Taylor, a drummer, remembered. "The squealing that he could do with that guitar was a piece of art."[41]

Hendrix also threw in every stage trick he had ever learned. He dressed exotically. He sported puffed-out, curly hair. In Harlem he would have been considered ridiculous. But in Greenwich Village, and especially at Café Wha?, which lacked a liquor license and thus drew a lot of white teenagers, he was mind-blowing.

Those teenagers did not realize it, but they were witnessing the birth of a rock legend.

Chapter 4

From Greenwich Village to Greenwich, England

At Richie Havens's urging, Mike Bloomfield, considered the best guitarist in New York, went to see "Jimmy James and the Blue Flames" at Café Wha? "H-bombs were going off, guided missiles were flying— I can't tell you the sounds he was getting out of his instrument," he said. "He was getting every sound I was ever to hear him get, right there in that room . . . I didn't even want to pick up a guitar for the next year."[1]

Blues musician John Hammond said, "Jimi amazed me. Playing left-handed and upside down on a Strat, he was *brilliant*. And offstage he was a sweet and essentially humble guy who took great joy in music. I recognized him as one of a kind."[2]

But producers were a harder sell. Linda Keith kept

trying to find one who would take on Hendrix. She was convinced he could be a star. Andrew Loog Oldham, the Rolling Stones' manager, would not bite. Neither would Seymour Stein of Sire Records.

"I was starting to doubt myself, and thinking I was mad," Keith said. Then, on July 5, 1966, she ran into Bryan "Chas" Chandler, the bass player for the English group The Animals ("House of the Rising Sun" was one of their biggest hits). Chandler, who planned to leave the band and take up producing, had recently heard a song called "Hey Joe" and was convinced that if he could find the right group to cover it, it would be a hit in England—and a great way to start his producing career.

"The Best Guitarist I'd Ever Seen"

Keith told Chandler there was a guitarist he should check out, and the two of them turned out for the Wednesday afternoon show at Café Wha? on August 3. Among the songs Hendrix played was his version of "Hey Joe." Chandler became so excited he spilled a milkshake on his suit. "I thought immediately he was the best guitarist I'd ever seen," he said.[3]

Chandler introduced himself to Hendrix and, as they talked, became convinced Hendrix could be a star. "I just sat there and thought to myself, 'There's got to be catch here.' I just couldn't believe that this guy was standing around and nobody was doing anything for him."[4]

Chandler asked Hendrix if he was signed with anyone. Hendrix said he would have to be bought out of a contract with Sue Records but failed to mention Ed Chalpin of PPX (a fact that would come back to haunt him). Chandler asked Hendrix if he would come to England. They shook hands on it, and Chandler said he would come back to iron out the details when the Animals' U.S. tour was over, in about five weeks. In the interim, Hendrix and the Blue Flames had a two-week gig at the Café Au Go Go.

Shortly thereafter, Linda Keith was taken back to England by her father. Keith Richards, lead guitarist of the Rolling Stones, with whom she had broken up, had told her father she was involved with a "black junkie" in New York.[5]

Without Linda Keith to help, it took Chas Chandler four days just to track Hendrix down when he returned to New York. Once he did, the two began planning the next stage of Hendrix's career.

The Animals were managed by Michael Jeffrey, and Chandler worked with him from the beginning. (As soon as Jeffrey saw Hendrix, even before he heard him play, he told Chandler, "*He* could be the black Elvis!")[6] The first problem was Hendrix's lack of a passport and papers that vouched for his reasons for entering the United Kingdom. Among other things, Hendrix needed a character reference—but all the people he knew well lived in Seattle. Chandler said later, "This New York writer I knew forged all the passport papers for us . . . like, 'Yes, I've known this man eight years, yes, he's a good character . . . '"[7]

Another forged document made it look like a U.K. promoter had asked Hendrix to make the trip. Meanwhile, Jeffrey put up the money (a few hundred dollars) to buy Hendrix's contract from Sue Records and arranged to get Hendrix's birth certificate from Seattle and for Hendrix to get the necessary vaccinations.

Hendrix assumed that Chandler wanted the Blue Flames as a group, but Chandler only wanted him. As it turned out, none of the Blue Flames either would or could accompany Hendrix. He asked Billy Cox to come along, but Cox also declined.

Sometime during this process, Chandler and Hendrix decided to change the spelling of his name from "Jimmy" to "Jimi." "Chas always liked to believe he had thought of it," Hendrix said. "Actually, that spelling had crossed my mind before; I'd even used it a couple of times in New York."[8]

At one point Hendrix, worried about becoming stranded in England, almost backed out. He asked Chandler, "What's the point in me coming to England as a guitar player? You've got Eric Clapton and Jeff Beck over there. You don't need one more guitar player." But, he said, "If you can guarantee that you'll introduce me to Clapton, I'll come to London." Chandler promised, and Hendrix made up his mind to go.[9]

Welcome to London

And so Jimi Hendrix arrived in London. To get him a work permit, Tony Garland, press officer for Michael Jeffrey, told immigration officials he was a famous singer coming to England to collect his royalties. After two hours of discussion, Hendrix received a one-week visa.

Chandler took Hendrix straight to the house of Zoot and Ronnie Money, active figures in London's club scene. Hendrix tried to play his electric guitar through the Moneys' stereo and could not, so instead he played someone's acoustic guitar. Later that night, Hendrix played at The Scotch of St. James, the most glamorous London night club of that era.

"They seemed to like me quite a lot," Hendrix said. "I felt overwhelmed inside that this was really happening. When I was wallowing in misery in New York, I'd imagine moments like this. But, quite naturally, I never could have dreamed that it all would happen in London, England."[10]

Kathy Etchingham, who was in the audience, remembered: "When we got there . . . there was Jimi and Chas and they all waved and said, 'over here.' So we all introduced ourselves and Jimi leaned over towards me and said, 'I want to tell you something,' and I said, 'What is it?' and I put my head forward. He kissed my ear and said, 'I think you're beautiful.'"[11] After the show, she and Hendrix went to Hendrix's hotel. They would be together, off and on, for the next two years.

In April of 1966, *Time* had put "Swinging London" on its cover. British bands—especially The Beatles— dominated charts all over the world. Frank Sinatra once sang about New York that "If I can make it there, I'll make it anywhere." In the pop music world of 1966, that was even more true of London.

Putting it Together

Hendrix set out to form a band while Michael Jeffrey worked through his extensive contacts (from members of Parliament to organized crime figures) to get Hendrix the work permit he needed to start playing in clubs.

Noel Redding, a twenty-year-old guitarist, saw an ad about auditions for the New Animals in the magazine *Melody Maker* and came to the Jeffrey-Chandler office. He was asked if he would be interested in joining Hendrix's band instead—and if he could play bass. "I said no, but I'd try," Redding remembered. He jammed with Hendrix. Hendrix said that Redding's hair reminded him of Bob Dylan, and hired him as the bass player.

The band only had two members, but Michael Jeffrey gave it a name: The Jimi Hendrix Experience. "We all thought it was wild, but then we really were 'an experience,'" Redding said.[12]

Hendrix wanted a nine-piece band, complete with horns, like the ones he knew from the Chitlin' Circuit. Chandler wanted a smaller group. In the end, Chandler's vision won out.

On October 1, Chandler kept his promise to introduce Hendrix to Eric Clapton. Hendrix and Chandler (and their girlfriends) attended a concert by Eric Clapton and Cream at the Polytechnic club. At the set break, Chandler called Clapton over and asked if Hendrix could jam with the band. Since Eric Clapton was considered the greatest guitarist in London at the time (a popular graffiti at the time was "Clapton is God"), Clapton and Cream were flabbergasted, but nevertheless, they let Hendrix up on stage.

Tony Garland, who had grown up around Clapton, recalled, "He got up there and played a killer version of Howlin' Wolf's 'Killin' Floor' . . . I knew what a fan [Clapton] was of Albert King, who had a slow version of that song. When Jimi started his take, though, it was about three times as fast as Albert King's version, and you could see Eric's jaw drop."[13]

Jimi Hendrix with Eric Clapton (right) some time in the late 1960s.

51

"Eric actually turned pale, he was so overwhelmed by Jimi's talent," Chandler said. "He could hardly talk."[14]

Jack Bruce, bass player for Cream, said later, "It must have been difficult for Eric to handle, because [Eric] was 'God,' and this unknown person comes along, and *burns*."[15]

A French singer named Johnny Hallyday heard Hendrix jamming in another club, Blaises, and asked him if he would like to open a couple of weeks' worth of shows on Hallyday's tour of France in October. Chandler thought that was exactly what the new band needed—except the "Jimi Hendrix Experience" did not exist yet, because it did not have a drummer. Chandler phoned a twenty-year-old drummer named John "Mitch" Mitchell who had just left another band (ironically, named the Blue Flames) and asked him to audition. The final choice, between Mitchell and a drummer named Aynsley Dunbar, was decided by a coin toss.[16]

The Experience begins

The Experience began rehearsals and signed contracts with Chandler and Jeffrey that stipulated the band would split 2.5 percent of all record royalties and Chandler and Jeffrey would get twenty percent of all income earned. Hendrix signed a separate contract giving Chandler half of his songwriting income for six years. Up front, each band member received fifteen pounds a week, an advance against future earnings. Hendrix, as usual, signed his contracts without reading them.

Hendrix used his new income to refurbish his wardrobe, buying an antique military jacket and several pairs of brightly colored velvet pants. He also began wearing a giant black cowboy hat. "Even before we knew his name, we called him 'that guy walking around who looks like he walked into a girl's closet and put everything on,'"[17] singer Terry Reid recalled.

Hendrix and Kathy Etchingham were living together in a cramped, expensive hotel room. When Etchingham complained to Ringo Starr (the Beatles' drummer) about it, he suggested they move into a two-bedroom apartment he owned at 34 Montague Square. Chandler and his girlfriend moved into it as well.

Hendrix tried to phone his father Al to tell him he was in England. He discovered Al had moved and had married a Japanese woman named Ayako Jinka who had five children. When he finally tracked his father down, as Etchingham remembered it, Al was furious that Jimi had called collect and would not believe that Jimi was in England. When Etchingham spoke to Al to convince him that Jimi really was overseas, Al said, "You tell my boy to write me. I ain't paying for no collect calls." And then he hung up.[18]

"I suppose to my dad, England seemed like another planet," Hendrix said. "He made me feel lousy. I always regretted making that call."[19]

The Jimi Hendrix Experience debuted opening for Johnny Hallyday in the Novelty Theatre in Evreux, France, playing just fifteen minutes. A French newspaper called Hendrix "a bad mixture of James Brown and Chuck Berry, who pulled a wry face onstage for a quarter of an hour and also played with his teeth."[20] It was not a promising beginning, but everything changed a few days later at the Olympia in Paris, before a crowd of 2,500.

French photographer Jean-Pierre Leloir remembered, "I was shocked by Jimi's way of playing, of behaving, onstage . . . Hendrix's music was disturbing. Different. He didn't pay attention at all to the camera. I immediately felt that he was going to be important . . . He was like a *butterfly* on that stage. All movement. *Natural.* Completely *natural*."[21]

Or, as Vic Briggs put it, "Jimi just wiped the floor with the crowd."[22]

"Hey Joe"

Exactly one month after Hendrix arrived in England, the Experience recorded its first single, "Hey Joe." Chandler wanted an original song for the flip side, so Hendrix wrote "Stone Free" in one evening.

Before the single came out, the band traveled to Germany, playing four nights at the Big Apple club in Munich. They played two shows a night, and the crowds grew with each show.

One night Hendrix, tossing his guitar back on stage after venturing into the crowd at the end of a long guitar cord, cracked the guitar's neck. Furious with himself, he grabbed the guitar, lifted it over his head, and smashed it on the stage. The crowd applauded wildly, and

Chandler decided then and there to have Hendrix smash more guitars in the future.

The Experience returned to England for more exposure in preparation for the release of "Hey Joe." They played small, low-paying venues, but excitement about the group grew, especially among other musicians. Pete Townshend of the Who first met Hendrix at a recording studio and was unimpressed, but once he heard him play, he said, "I became an immediate fan. I saw all of Jimi's first London shows."[23] Brian Jones of the Rolling Stones started dragging other stars to Hendrix's shows.

Hendrix turned twenty-four on November 27, 1966. On December 16 "Hey Joe" was released by Track Records, a new label started by Kit Lambert and Chris Stamp, who also managed the Who. (Decca and at least two other record labels had rejected it; Decca said

One Bandleader to Another

When Little Richard came to town in December of 1966, Hendrix and Kathy Etchingham went to see him. Hendrix was pleased to be able to meet his former boss on a bandleader-to-bandleader basis, and they had a pleasant evening until an argument erupted over $50 Hendrix claimed Little Richard owed him. Little Richard denied owing anything but did give Hendrix the money in the end.

As Hendrix and Kathy walked home, seven policemen surrounded them and forced Jimi to remove his antique military jacket. "Do you realize that our soldiers died in that uniform?" one shouted. The police told Hendrix if they saw him wearing the jacket again they would arrest him. As soon as they were out of sight, he put it back on.[24]

Hendrix was "lacking in long-term potential."[25]) One reason Chandler signed Hendrix with Track Records was that Lambert and Stamp guaranteed the Experience a spot on the influential TV show *Ready, Steady, Go!*, where the Rolling Stones, the Animals, the Kinks, and the Moody Blues had all made their TV debuts.[26]

The Experience played on TV just before "Hey Joe" was released, and the song became an immediate hit—with a little help from Hendrix's management, which sent people out to all the record shops, buying up copies to push the single up the charts. "It's called payola, and I know it happened because I bought several of them myself," Etchingham later said.[27]

Working on an Album

That winter, while recording its first album, the Experience played all over England to raise money for studio time, often rushing back to London in the middle of the night to record when studio time was cheaper. (To keep costs down, Chandler often recorded "rehearsal," then surprised the musicians by telling them he already had a master track.)

On January 11, the band recorded all day, laying down (among others) "Purple Haze," inspired by a dream Hendrix had that, in turn, was inspired by a science fiction novel: *Night of Light: Day of Dreams*, by Philip Jose Farmer.

That night they performed two shows at the Bag O' Nails. An extraordinary collection of rock stars attended, but perhaps just as importantly, so did an electronics

"The Wind Cries Mary"

Hendrix wrote a song every other day in January, 1967. Some he had been working on for more than a year, others were brand-new.

"The Wind Cries Mary," one of Hendrix's most enduring hits, resulted from a fight Hendrix and Kathy Etchingham (whose middle name was Mary) had over her cooking. She stormed out for the night. When she returned the next day, the song was finished.

It was recorded in twenty minutes at the end of a session. "We simply didn't rehearse," Redding said. "Jimi just basically played the chords, and being an ex-guitar player, I could pick up the stuff really fast, and we got the feel, and we put it down."[28]

genius named Roger Mayer. Mayer was working for the Royal Navy Scientific Service on sound distortion, and developed effects boxes for guitar players in his spare time.[29] He was so impressed that later he would make effects boxes strictly for Hendrix. "Hendrix was playing and I was floored," he said. "It was like everything I had ever imagined."[30]

Hendrix's fellow musicians continued to praise his playing. "We got a tremendous amount of help from people like Mick Jagger, Paul McCartney, and John Lennon," Chandler remembered. "They would rave about Hendrix and turn the entire course of an interview around just to talk about him."[31]

At the end of January the Experience played two shows at the Saville Theatre with the Who. Paul McCartney, John Lennon, and George Harrison of the Beatles attended, as did the members of Cream. In fact, Jack

Bruce of Cream left the theater after one show so inspired by Hendrix's performance that he promptly wrote the famous and instantly recognizable opening riff for "Sunshine of Your Love," one of Cream's biggest hits.[32]

The Experience finished the album that spring and called it *Are You Experienced*. Before it was released, the band did a tour of English movie theaters, as part of a revue that included Cat Stevens and Engelbert Humperdinck and headlined the Walker Brothers.

Are You Experienced?

In a magazine article that March, Hendrix listed "music, hair, mountains, and fields" as likes; "marmalade and cold sheets" as dislikes; "reading science fiction, painting landscapes, daydreaming, and music" as hobbies; Bob Dylan, Muddy Waters, and Mozart as his favorite composers; and strawberry shortcake and spaghetti as his favorite foods. His personal ambition, he said, was "to have my own style of music."[33]

A Fiery Performance

On the first night of the tour, a journalist, Keith Altham, was talking to Hendrix and Chas Chandler about what Hendrix could do to make himself stand out. "It is a pity," Altham said, "that you can't set your guitar on fire."[34]

Hendrix immediately got hold of some lighter fluid and began experimenting. That night, at the end of the Experience's five-song set (the final song was, naturally, "Fire"), he poured lighter fluid on his guitar and threw a match at it. It burst into flames (on the third attempt) and became a rock music legend.[35]

He was realizing that ambition. *Are You Experienced* made it to number two on the British charts, behind the Beatles' *Sgt. Pepper's Lonely Hearts Club Band*. Keith Altham wrote in *New Musical Express* that "Hendrix is a new dimension in electrical guitar music, launching what amounts to a one-man assault upon the nerve cells. The LP [album] is a brave effort by Hendrix to produce a musical form which is original and exciting."[36]

But more important for Hendrix's career were two other developments. In March, Michael Jeffrey had signed a deal with Warner Bros. for the release of *Are You Experienced* in the United States, for a then-record $150,000, equivalent to about $850,000 today.[37] ("A massive campaign hailing Jimi Hendrix as 'the greatest talent since the Rolling Stones is being launched in America," wrote the *New Musical Express* on March 18, 1967.[38])

And in California, Lou Adler, a producer, and John Phillips, a member of the Mamas and the Papas, were organizing a music festival for Monterey, California, scheduled for June 16, 17, and 18. Paul McCartney and Andrew Loog Oldham, the British advisors for the festival, picked the Experience and the Who as the most important British acts to have on the bill.

When Chandler told Hendrix, he said, "I'm going home."[39]

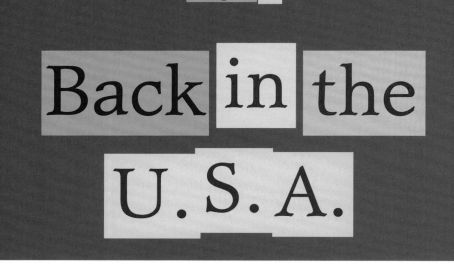

Chapter 5

Back in the U.S.A.

Before heading to the United States, the Experience had a few more concerts to play—and a new album to begin, even though *Are You Experienced* had just come out. *Axis: Bold as Love* came together quickly, thanks to hard work in the studio. "Chas came from the old school of, 'We've got four hours, let's make the most of it,'" Eddie Kramer, who engineered the album, remembered.[1]

Hendrix's technological experiments complicated things. Electronics expert Roger Mayer recalled, "Jimi was always asking me, 'Roger, what can we do?' We were trying to use sounds to create emotions and paint pictures. We had only crude technology at the time, but if we didn't have something we'd build it."[2]

When technology did not work for Hendrix—and it often did not, since the Experience's extremely loud playing damaged amplifiers, and Hendrix's extensive use of the tremolo bar led to tuning problems—he could lose his temper. On May 29 in Spaulding he swore at a four-thousand-strong audience after it jeered him for taking several breaks to tune. Germaine Greer wrote in *Oz*, "They . . . didn't even care whether 'Hey Joe' was in tune or not. They just wanted to hear something and adulate . . . but Jimi wanted, like he always wanted, to play it sweet and high. So he did it . . . and they moaned and swayed about, and he looked at them heavily and knew that they couldn't hear what he was trying to do and never would."[3]

Farewell, England

On June 4, the Experience played two "farewell England" shows at the Saville Theatre. Since the Beatles' manager, Brian Epstein, owned the Saville, there was a possibility the Beatles would attend, making their first appearance since the release of *Sgt. Pepper's Lonely Hearts Club Band* just three days earlier.

Sure enough, when the Experience came on stage, Paul McCartney and George Harrison were sitting in Epstein's box. Hendrix thanked everyone for coming and then launched into his opening number: "Sgt. Pepper's Lonely Hearts Club Band."

He had burst into the dressing room just thirty minutes earlier and announced to Redding and Mitchell it would be the first song. "We thought he'd gone daft," Redding recalled.[4] Hendrix played the song off the album a few times so his bandmates could learn the chords, and then they had gone on. "It was basically done just off the cuff, but that's how we did everything," said Redding. "We were fearless."

"The Beatles couldn't believe it," engineer Eddie Kramer remembered. "Here was Hendrix playing a song off their album that had just come out, and he'd taken the song and figured out a completely new arrangement, which was killer."[5]

It could have been a career-ending embarrassment if they'd produced an inferior version of the song; but they did not. Paul McCartney called hearing the Experience play "Sgt. Pepper's" that night "one of the greatest honors of my career."[6]

Hendrix ended the concert by smashing a guitar he had hand-painted with a poem dedicated to Britain, then kicking the pieces into the audience. That night, when they showed up at Brian Epstein's home for an after-show supper party, Paul McCartney was at the door to welcome them in.[7]

Two weeks after the "farewell England" concerts, the Experience, Brian Jones, and Eric Burdon flew from London to New York for a short layover before flying on to California for the Monterey Festival. When the Experience checked into the Chelsea Hotel, a woman thought Hendrix was a bellhop and wanted him to carry her bags. The band checked right back out again.

Backstage at Monterey Pop

The next day the band flew to San Francisco to spend the night. Hendrix had not been there since he had been stationed at Fort Ord six years earlier.

San Francisco in 1967 was very different from San Francisco in 1961. It was the "Summer of Love," and thousands of young people had moved into the Haight district. Snappy dressing was the rage in Swingin' London, but in San Francisco, long hair, jeans, and beads were the standard costume. Demonstrations for civil rights and against the Vietnam War were occurring regularly across the country. Anarchist groups like the Yippies and the Diggers demanded, among other things, that music festivals—including The First International Festival of Music in Monterey, the Experience's destination—should be free.[8]

The goal of the weekend-long Monterey Pops Festival (as it was more informally known), was to make rock 'n' roll as culturally respected as jazz (the annual Monterey Jazz Festival, first held in 1958, was already legendary). The organizers had planned for 10,000 fans to descend on the Marin County Fairgrounds; instead, at least 90,000 turned up. To keep them entertained, alternative stages for jam sessions were set up outside the main festival gates.

Hendrix had a chance to meet with and talk to a number of other performers before the Experience's Sunday-night concert. Late Saturday Hendrix borrowed a guitar and played for a while on an alternative stage, surrounded by people sleeping. "People in the crowd actually groaned when they saw him because no one knew who he was, and they wanted to get some sleep," Eric Burdon remembered. "He started playing this beautiful, sad, melodic stuff, and it developed into a happy jam."[9] Other musicians from bands like the Grateful Dead and Jefferson Airplane joined him.

The next day, Hendrix jammed backstage during the Grateful Dead's concert. At one point Hendrix, Janis Joplin, Mama Cass of the Mamas and the Papas, Roger Daltrey of the Who, Eric Burdon, and Brian Jones were all singing "Sgt. Pepper's Lonely Hearts Club Band," until a promoter came down from the stage and told them to shut up because they were making too much noise.[10]

The Sunday line-up was undefined, except that sitarist Ravi Shankar would open the show and the Mamas

Summer of Love . . . or Acid?

One of the people backstage at the Monterey Pop Festival was Augustus Owsley Stanley III. Stanley, a financial supporter and sometimes sound man for the Grateful Dead, was an "underground chemist" who made between 100 thousand and 10 million doses of LSD in his home laboratory (for which he soon spent three years in prison).[11] At Monterey, he handed out free samples, which, because they were purple, were nicknamed "purple haze" by people who had heard Hendrix's song.

"They call it the Summer of Love," Hendrix said later. "Summer of Acid is more like it! The LSD passed around in San Francisco was a fabulous discovery to me. I'd taken LSD in London, but this acid was advanced, a whole other thing. I wanted more; it became the great escape . . . I overdid it. I know that now. Almost every musician I knew was an acid freak."[12]

Many of those musicians, including Hendrix, went on to suffer serious consequences because of their drug habits.

and the Papas would close it. Hendrix did not want to follow the Who; the Who did not want to follow the Experience. A coin toss finally decided the matter. Hendrix lost. "If I'm going to follow you," Hendrix warned Pete Townshend, "I'm going to pull out all the stops."[13]

Smashing Successes

The Who gave a fantastic show that launched their fame in America. As usual, Townshend smashed his guitar at the end, sending bits flying thirty feet or more. Rock critic Ellen Sander said, "Nobody would sit down. A shiver of apprehension snaked through the air. There was a feeling of something uncontrollable with all its good and frightening implications."[14]

The Grateful Dead went on next, their laid-back sound relaxing the crowd a bit before the final act. Brian Jones of the Rolling Stones introduced the Experience: "I'd like to introduce you to a very good friend, a fellow countryman of yours . . . A brilliant performer, the most exciting guitarist I've ever heard: the Jimi Hendrix Experience."[15]

Hendrix came on wearing a yellow ruffled shirt, his military jacket, tight red pants, and a headband. He played behind his back, between his legs, and with his teeth. By the third song, "Like a Rolling Stone," "you would have seen thousands of Os because everyone's mouth was open," said Paul Body, who was in the crowd. "We'd never heard anything like it, and we'd never seen anything like him."[16]

Michael Lydon, a founding editor of *Rolling Stone*, wrote, "Hendrix did not only pick the strings, he bashed them with the flat of his hand, he ripped at them, rubbed them against the mike, and pushed them . . . into his amplifier."[17]

"We destroyed the place. We just nailed it," said Redding. "That made the band in America."[18]

The show ended with "Wild Thing." Before launching into it, Hendrix said, "I'm going to sacrifice something right here that I really love. Don't think I'm silly doing this because I don't think I'm losing my mind. This is the only way I can do it."[19] Two minutes into the song, Hendrix doused his guitar in lighter fluid, set it on fire, and then smashed the flaming instrument.

The whole thing was captured on film by D.A. Pennebaker.

Pete Johnson wrote in the *Los Angeles Times* that by the end of that performance "the Jimi Hendrix Experience owned the future, and the audience knew it in an instant. When Jimi left the stage he graduated from rumor to legend."[20]

"Our band was great," Hendrix enthused. "It was like the birthday you always dream of and it never happens."[21]

Hey, Hey, We're the Experience

The Experience was on the verge of U.S. fame but did not have a lot of bookings yet. After Monterey they played the Fillmore in San Francisco, originally opening for a bill that included Janis Joplin, and then headlining when promoter Bill Graham saw how great the response was.[22] In July, the group moved to the Whisky A Go Go, where stars like Mama Cass (of the Mamas and the Papas) and Jim Morrison (of the Doors) turned out.

The next day, the Experience flew to New York. They played two clubs, then flew to Jacksonville, Florida, to start one of the oddest concert tours of all time, opening for the made-for-TV pop band The Monkees. Michael Jeffrey had arranged it; Chandler thought he was nuts.

Stan Cornyn, a Warner Brothers executive, recalled that "in those days (at Reprise) anything beyond Dean Martin fell into one category. And the Monkees and Jimi Hendrix were beyond Dean Martin. So nobody at the time in Burbank had any feelings of absurdity in pairing them. After all, they both played loud."[23]

"Our audience didn't exactly dig him," said Peter Tork of the Monkees. But the Monkees did. "We'd get there early and watch him from backstage. What he did was simply exquisite. I loved to watch the way his hands worked—it came so easily to him it looked as if he wasn't playing at all."[24]

Besides, said Mickey Dolenz, "We all had a lot of fun in the hotels. The Monkees were into chicks and being drunk and stoned and stuff, and so was Jimi's band. But . . . when the Monkees were on stage, we had to do 'Last Train to Clarksville.'"

He added, "It was driving the Experience crazy to play for kids as young as eight and ten after their incredible reception from teenagers and adults in

Devon Wilson

According to biographer Charles R. Cross, Hendrix met Devon Wilson at a party in Laurel Canyon in July of 1967. By some other accounts, he had already met her before he left New York.

Devon Wilson's real name was Ida Mae Wilson. Devon was the name she used while working as a street prostitute, after running out west from Milwaukee at the age of fifteen. By 1967 she was a rock "super groupie," heavily into drugs. For three years, she and Hendrix had an on-again, off-again relationship.[25]

According to Alan Douglas, Devon "understood music, she was very strong, very opinionated. Devon had lesbian tendencies, she had drug tendencies . . . so that I don't think she had the sensitivity to be the female that Hendrix had in mind as his ideal female. But she was the only one that I have ever seen, you know, get up in his face and tell him when he was . . . not playing right and he respected her, he respected her a lot."

Later on, when she got more heavily into cocaine and heroin, Hendrix would be more suspicious of her, Douglas said, but "she influenced the business . . . she kept all the fools away from him, she was very protective and when the day was over she was a very good friend and served in lots of capacities."

Including, unfortunately for Hendrix, drug supplier.[26]

Monterey. The little kids didn't understand their music."[27]

Hendrix complained to Chandler, who got the Experience off the tour after eight shows—then issued a press release claiming Hendrix had been kicked off the tour because the Daughters of the American Revolution had complained his show was "too erotic" (sexually charged). That led to great publicity like the *New Music Express* headline "Hendrix: Did He Quit or Was He Pushed?"[28]

Back in New York

Back in New York, the Experience played in various clubs and Hendrix caught up with friends. He still could not get any respect in Harlem; his friends the Aleems arranged for him to meet an influential black DJ named Frankie Crocker, but Crocker hated *Are You Experienced*. And Hendrix's clothes were still too wild for Harlem. But in Greenwich Village, some people had heard his singles and treated him like a star.

The Experience did a few more shows in the United States in August, then returned to England. On September 1, 1967, *Are You Experienced* was released in the United States. While crossing the Atlantic, the album picked up a question mark, becoming *Are You Experienced?*, and also exchanged "Red House," "Can You See Me," and "Remember" for the three singles that had been released in the United Kingdom: "Hey Joe," "Purple Haze," and "The Wind Cries Mary."

Reviews were mostly positive. *Are You Experienced?* became one of the fastest sellers in the history of Reprise records, outselling Frank Sinatra—once one of Hendrix's musical heroes.

On September 16, 1967, *Melody Maker* named Jimi Hendrix "World's Best Pop Musician" at its annual awards party at the Hotel Europa in London. A few days

The Strangest Session

One of the oddest things Hendrix did during this time was to drop by, at 2:00 A.M., the apartment of Ed Chalpin, with whom he had once signed a contract. Based on that contract, Chalpin had been trying to get a court to halt any future recordings by the Experience. Nevertheless, Hendrix asked if he could borrow money to take his old band-mate Curtis Knight to dinner. The three ended up going to dinner together, and Chalpin did loan Hendrix some money. Afterward, still in the middle of the night, Hendrix went into the studio and recorded six tracks for Chalpin.

"I just wanted to cool everybody out," Hendrix later explained. "I said I'd play on some tracks for Curtis but that they couldn't use my name. Curtis agreed."[29] Even though Chalpin *did* release the tracks, complicating legal matters further, in August Hendrix did *another* session for him with Curtis Knight.[30]

later the banner headline appeared in ads from Track Records: "All Hail King Jimi!"

A few days before, Hendrix said, "We were off somewhere on the road, and I was brushing my teeth, thinking about it. I started to cry because it meant so much, and I ended up washing my face three times to get off this mess of tears and toothpaste." He added, "Nineteen sixty-seven was the best year of my life."[31]

Axis: Bold as Love

By the end of October *Axis: Bold as Love* was finished. Many of the songs had a science-fiction theme or feel, partly due to Roger Mayer's inventions. "I spent a lot of time with Jimi privately, hanging out and talking about the sounds and maybe bringing a few boxes around the flat so he could jam in private. And we would get some general ideas of what we were trying to accomplish in the way of sustain and tone. We were normally using colours to describe the sound," Mayer said.[32]

"There was nothing we wouldn't do, or that we wouldn't want to try for him," engineer Eddie Kramer said. "The rules were there were no rules."[33]

"We've tried to get most of the freaky tracks right

Jimi Hendrix's many stage theatrics are legendary, including playing his guitar with his teeth (above).

into another dimension so you get that sky-effect, like they're coming down out of the heavens," Hendrix explained.[34]

Despite his success, Hendrix was insecure about his singing voice. He would make everyone clear out of the studio and have the lights dimmed before he recorded his vocal track. At the end of "Spanish Castle Magic" he muttered, "I can't sing a song."[35]

The new album came out in the United Kingdom on December 1, 1967, and in the United States one month later. The *Melody Maker* review said, "Amaze your ears, boggle your mind, flip your lid, do what you want but please get into Hendrix like you never have before."[36]

Not long before *Axis: Bold As Love* came out, Hendrix turned twenty-five. He did not have much time to celebrate: he was in the middle of an English tour that saw the Experience do thirty-two shows in twenty-two days. The brutal pace of touring and recording finally began to tell on the band as 1967 wound down. In an interview with Bob Farmer of *Disc*, Hendrix said, "I know we'll have to

"An Unending Revolt Against Convention"

In *Jimi Hendrix: Electric Gypsy*, Harry Shapiro and Caesar Glebbeek point to *Axis: Bold As Love* as an example of why Jimi Hendrix is seen as the consummate rebel.

"One reviewer of the album asked how a man as gentle as Jimi could produce such violent music," they write. "But this is at the core of romanticism: an unending revolt against convention, authoritarianism, insincerity and moderation, an extreme assertion of the self, a celebration of the value of individual experience."[37]

change some way, but I don't know how to do it. I suppose this staleness will finish us in the end."[38]

Drunk and disorderly

On the first day of a January tour of Scandinavia Hendrix got drunk and trashed his hotel room, injured his hand in the process, and was arrested. He was soon released, but he had to pay a fine, and the legal costs soaked up a full third of the band's earnings from the tour. As well, the headlines were embarrassing. (Rock stars trashing hotel rooms were still a novelty in those days.)

Also taking its toll on the band was the increasing intake of drugs by all three musicians. According to Redding, it had become a game of "I can take more than you."[39]

Finally, at the end of January, the Experience returned to the United States, where *Are You Experienced?* had sold over a million copies. However, reviews for *Axis: Bold As Love* were not great. Many critics focused solely on Hendrix's guitar playing. They were less impressed with his songwriting or his singing. Hendrix did not help the album when, in an interview with Michael Rosenbaum of *Crawdaddy*, he said he only liked three songs on it: "Bold As Love," "Little Wing," and "Little Miss Lover." The next album, he said, would have to be made his way "or else."[40]

Home to Seattle

The tour started in San Francisco, where, at one point, Hendrix headlined over blues guitar great Albert King, one of his old idols. The shows drew rave reviews, and demonstrated Hendrix's appeal across racial lines. According to promoter Bill Graham, Hendrix was the "first black sex symbol in White America."[41]

After a few more dates in California, the tour moved to Hendrix's old home town of Seattle, where the Experience was booked for a sold-out February 12 show at the Seattle Center Arena.

Hendrix had not been home for seven years. When he got off the plane, Leon, Al, and Al's new wife and her children were waiting to meet him. "He had on this giant hat, and a red velvet shirt. He had all this hair and he looked just wild!" Leon recalled.

Hendrix told one interviewer he was afraid his father would grab him and cut off his hair. Instead, Al took Jimi's hand, put his other hand on his back, and said, "Welcome home, son."[42]

Jimi spent the rest of the afternoon at Al's house. Among the friends and family who dropped by were Aunt Delores and Dorothy Harding. "He looked so grown up," Delores said. "He was like a hippie!"[43] But other friends, including Terry Johnson and Jimmy Williams, were not there: they were serving in Vietnam.

Hendrix asked Ernestine Benson to curl his hair before that night's concert. "The problem with my life today," he told her, "is that I have to take a pill to sleep, and a pill to perform."

"You got to take some time off," she told him.[44]

Hendrix's family sat in the front row that night (in

front of the speakers—Al had his fingers in his ears part of the time). In his review in *Helix*, Tom Robbins wrote, "Hendrix is a hotly exciting performer. What he lacks in content, he makes up in style. He is, in fact, a master stylist; an outrageous exponent of high black showmanship . . . and freaking fine."[45]

Return to Garfield High

A week before the show the promoter, Pat O'Day, asked Hendrix if he wanted to do anything special in Seattle. Hendrix said he wanted to play a free show for Garfield High School students. But after the show, Hendrix stayed up all night, drinking with his brother and playing Monopoly. When journalist Patrick MacDonald arrived at Al's house at 7:30 A.M. to pick up Jimi (without Redding, Mitchell, or a roadie—O'Day had not been able to wake any of them up), Hendrix had not slept, showered, or changed since the previous night's performance, and he was hung over.

"He was not capable, or able, to play, or really to speak," Garfield principal Frank Fidler remembered. Instead, they decided to just have Hendrix give a talk, then answer questions. However, most of the students were black, and they did not know who Hendrix was, because his music was not played on black radio. They did not like his "hippie" style of dress, either.

Faced with a restless, heckling crowd, Hendrix mumbled, "I've been here, and there, and everywhere, and it's all working," paused, then said he had written

"Purple Haze" for Garfield, whose school colors were purple and white. And that was his speech.

The question-and-answer session was not much better. Asked how long he had been gone from Garfield, he replied, "Oh, about 2,000 years." Then, asked "How do you write a song?" Hendrix looked at the floor, then said, "Right now, I'm going to say goodbye to you, and go out the door, and get into my limousine, and go to the airport. And when I get out the door, the assembly will be over, and the bell will ring. And when I hear that bell ring, I'll write a song. Thank you very much." He walked out to a chorus of boos. "I just can't face an audience without my guitar," Hendrix told O'Day and MacDonald. "I don't feel well."

"It was so strange how bad the whole thing turned out," O'Day said later. "It had all been his idea. He had wanted so badly to go back to the school he'd gone to. It was supposed to have been a homecoming. When he got there he was scared."[46]

Eulogy for a Hero

A few weeks later in Ottawa, Ontario, by a twist of fate, the Monkees opened for the Experience. Hendrix made what would become his standard reference to the Vietnam War: "Instead of all that action happening over there, why doesn't everyone just come on home, and instead of M16 machine guns, hand grenades and tanks on their backs, why don't they come back with feedback guitars on their backs? That's better than guns."[47]

Hendrix also enjoyed some time in Ottawa with

Canadian-born singer Joni Mitchell, whom he had met in Greenwich Village.

In Cleveland in March, Hendrix dropped by a Chevrolet dealership and bought a brand-new 1968 Corvette Stingray for $8,000 in cash (about $45,000 today[48])— even though he did not have a driver's license (and had such poor vision he could never have gotten one without wearing glasses, which he refused to do), or any place to keep a car. He convinced a salesmen to drive the car to New York, where his management would store it.[49]

On April 4, 1968, civil rights proponent Dr. Martin Luther King Jr.—a hero to many Americans, and especially to African Americans—was assassinated in Memphis, Tennessee. The next day, as they arrived in Newark, New Jersey, the Experience saw an armored vehicle and wondered if war had broken out. (In fact, riots were predicted in Newark. Their white limousine driver was so scared he refused to drive unless Hendrix sat up front with him.)

At Newark Symphony Hall, the police ordered Hendrix to only play one of the two scheduled shows. Only four hundred people showed up by show time. "This number is for a friend of mine," Hendrix said, and began a mournful blues instrumental.

"The music had a kind of appalling beauty," said Mark Boyle, who was running the lights for Soft Machine, also on the bill. "Harrowing music."[50]

The improvisational show, punctuated by gunshots outside, ended without applause. The following week, without any fanfare, Hendrix donated $5,000 to a memorial fund in Dr. King's honor.[51]

Friction in the Band

Despite good record sales and large crowds, the band needed more cash. That meant they needed a third album—but it was coming along slowly, partly because of Hendrix's experimentation. Jack Adams, an engineer at the Record Plant in New York, remembered: "He'd have such a set idea of what he wanted a record to sound like that he'd remix a song 300 times. No fooling. We'd remix a song for ten hours, all night, all week. I'd get tired and say . . . I'm going home . . . Then, about ten the next morning, the janitors would phone up and say, 'Hey, get this guy outta here, we gotta clean the place up.'"

The hours and hours spent recording, plus the fact that Hendrix brought in many extra musicians to add color and variety, created friction in the band. Redding hated sitting around all day while Hendrix experimented and remixed and rerecorded. He also resented the other musicians—and that Hendrix did not take any of his suggestions or show much interest in his songs (although one did eventually make it onto the album).[52]

Mitch Mitchell was frustrated, too. He later said they could have worked on the record for a year and it would not have been finished to Hendrix's satisfaction.[53]

All of which contributed to the fact that, when it finally came out in 1968, *Electric Ladyland* would prove to be the last album by the Jimi Hendrix Experience.

Chapter 6

Electric Ladyland

The Experience's bruising tour schedule continued.
At the beginning of May, they got a little time in the
studio. Then they were off to the Miami Pop Festival
and to Europe for a short tour of Italy and Switzerland.
This was interrupted for Hendrix by a couple of days of
legal meetings in New York, where the old contract with
Ed Chalpin continued to be a problem. In June, they
finally had a few more days to work on the new album.
And around the same time, Chas Chandler quit as
Hendrix's producer.

"Jimi Doesn't Listen to Me"

"This is not the life I want," Chandler told journalist
Sharon Lawrence. "Jimi is now completely surrounded
by hangers-on, particularly when we're in New York. I
can't stand 'em! I'm not putting up with this! . . . Jimi
doesn't listen to me or anyone else."[1]

Chandler was also fed up with Hendrix's drug use.
"Drugs didn't get in the way of shows and it didn't get

in the way of recording, but I thought it was getting in the way of his brain. . . . It had to stop."[2]

Chandler claimed he also quit as Hendrix's co-manager, but Trixie Sullivan, Chandler and Jeffrey's office manager, said Hendrix was given a choice: Chandler or Michael Jeffrey. He chose Jeffrey. "Chas never forgave him for that," she said. Jeffrey bought out Chandler for $300,000.[3]

Hendrix biographers Harry Shapiro and Caesar Glebbeek call that "a major miscalculation" on Hendrix's part. As a businessman, they wrote, Jeffrey's "prime directive was making money and the means of achieving this as far as Mike was concerned—lots of touring and quickly produced commercial records—was fundamentally at odds with the way Jimi wanted to work."[4]

There were also concerns about whether the band's money was being looked after properly. "Jimi knew there were problems, but he always had what he needed. . . . The bills just went straight to the office."[5]

As journalist Keith Altham said, "It's easy to make Mike Jeffery the villain of the piece but he didn't pretend to be much more than what he was—a business-oriented manager. Jimi elected to have that kind of representation and when he lost Chas, he lost a very important part of his direction and care."[6]

Hendrix, Kathy Etchingham, Chandler, and Chandler's girlfriend still lived together; that had to change. Etchingham leased a new apartment in the Mayfair neighborhood. It took up two floors above a street-level café in an old house next door to one where composer George Frederic Handel once lived. That impressed Hendrix. He did not know much about Handel, except that he was a famous composer, but while he and Etchingham were shopping for furniture and other decorations for the new apartment, he took time to buy recordings of Handel's organ concertos.[7]

Building Electric Ladyland

Back in New York, Hendrix and Jeffrey planned to turn a defunct nightclub called the Generation Club at 52 West Eighth into a recording studio. Owning their own studio would put an end to the enormous studio bills for recording *Electric Ladyland*—the third Experience album. The necessity of paying those bills also kept the Experience focused on touring the United States. "America is where the big money is," said Mitch Mitchell.[8]

But money slipped through their fingers like water. "Jimi might spend ten thousand dollars in a boutique on a girl he just met, and then never see her again," Sullivan remembered. Limousine and restaurant bills alone cost thousands every month. Legal expenses from the battle with Ed Chalpin cost thousands more.[9]

The Experience's second U.S. tour began at the end of July in Baton Rouge, Louisiana. The racial prejudice they encountered in the Deep South horrified and enraged Mitchell and Redding, but Hendrix took it more or less in stride. At one concert, promoter Pat O'Day remembered, a police officer "protecting" Hendrix pulled a gun on him when he saw him with a white girl.

The moment passed, but afterward the entire security force "left the show because they couldn't stand the idea of a black man with this white girl," O'Day said. He was furious, but Hendrix said, "Fifty years ago, I couldn't have even walked into this auditorium. And fifty years from now, no one is going to care."[10]

In September, the tour reached Seattle. Hendrix partied with Leon, angering Al. "We came home real late," said Leon, "and the house was still full of people waiting for Jimi to show up. My dad was waiting in the doorway holding his belt in his hand. He said, 'You boys go in the room, you're getting a whipping for this.'" Al did not actually whip them—how could he?—but he remained angry all night.[11]

Hendrix drove with his family to the next show in Vancouver, British Columbia, in a new car he had recently bought Al. Hendrix's grandmother Nora attended the show, and he dedicated "Foxy Lady" to her. She told a reporter, "The way he was picking that guitar, oh, my gracious! I don't see how he could stand all that noise."[12]

California Dreaming

When the tour got back to Los Angeles a few days later, the Experience finally had a bit of a break—Hendrix's first in two years. He rented a mansion in Benedict Canyon that had been used by other touring rock bands, including the Rolling Stones. The band did some recording and had a few shows. The rest of the time Hendrix slept late and went out to the clubs at night with a new companion, a waitress named Carmen

Borrero (she had once been a Playboy bunny—a server at a Playboy club). His brother Leon joined him, enjoying his big brother's endless supply of drugs and groupies.

Sepp Donahower, a concert promoter, described the house as "noisy . . . crawling with creepy people. Jimi was at least a little stoned, and I could tell he just wanted some peace and quiet, and here was a bunch of people partying and making themselves at home in a house he was paying for . . . finally he just burst loose. He yelled and cursed and told them all to get [out]."[13]

While in Denver on September 2, Hendrix wrote out

A Nasty Drunk

Though generally gentle and soft-spoken, Hendrix had a nasty temper that surfaced when he drank, especially when the drink was combined with drugs—which it pretty much always was.

Once when the house was broken into and Hendrix's guitars, clothes, and a book of lyrics were stolen, he accused an old friend, Paul Caruso, of the theft, punched him in the stomach, and chased him down the hill, throwing rocks and sticks at him. "Bash him in the face," Redding advised Caruso when he found out. "He's got it coming."[14]

Another time Hendrix accused Carmen Borrero of being involved with Eric Burdon and threw an empty vodka bottle at her, hitting her above her eye. "They had to rush me to the hospital, and they were afraid I was going to lose my eye," she said.

"It was the beginning of a seed of tragedy because he started lashing out at other people," said Eric Burdon.

"You wouldn't expect somebody with that kind of love to be that violent," said another friend, Herbie Worthington. "He just couldn't drink."[15]

detailed instructions on what he wanted for the cover for *Electric Ladyland*, including photographs by Linda Eastman (later to marry Paul McCartney and become better known as Linda McCartney) and liner notes. (The title came from his name for groupies: "Electric Ladies."[16]) The label ignored most of his suggestions.

The double album *Electric Ladyland* was released on September 17 in the United States and rocketed to the top of the Billboard charts. "All Along the Watchtower," a cover version of a Bob Dylan song, became the Experience's best-selling single ever in the United States. Some critics said it was the only cover of a Bob Dylan song that was better than the Bob Dylan original.[17]

The English version of the album cover was supposed to feature Hendrix surrounded by women. Hendrix did not like the idea and did not show up for the photo shoot, so the women were instead paid more money to take off their clothes. The resulting cover produced lots of publicity, but also resulted in the album being covered in a plain brown wrapper in some stores. This may be why it only made it to the fifth position on the U.K. charts.

Despite the album's success in the United States, not all critics were won over. Some thought the double album was too long. Hendrix countered by saying he would have preferred a triple album. "We really got about half of what we wanted to say in it," he said.[18]

Looking to Make a Change

As 1969 began, Hendrix began talking about wanting to do something different. To *Melody Maker*, he said, "Very soon . . . we'll be breaking the group apart for selected dates."[19]

Redding and Hendrix were not getting along at all by then. (Mitchell mostly just tried to keep his head down in the ongoing battles.) While in Los Angeles, Hendrix told journalist Sharon Lawrence, "Noel Redding's driving me crazy, just a stuck-on-himself English guitar player." She suggested the problems were just a result of their rather sudden fame. Fame, Hendrix agreed, "takes a *lot* of getting used to."[20]

Redding later agreed. "We were so overwhelmed by the money and the glamour of being so-called pop stars, we all forgot we were people."[21]

> **"[Fame] takes a *lot* of getting used to."**
>
> **—Jimi Hendrix**

Hendrix stayed in New York for a while after the 1968 U.S. tour ended, only returning to the United Kingdom on January 2, 1969. One thing he did upon his return was publicly identify Kathy Etchingham for the first time, two years into their relationship, as "my girlfriend, my past girlfriend and probably my future girlfriend. . . . My Yoko Ono from Chester."[22] (Yoko Ono was the soon-to-be wife of John Lennon of the Beatles.)

The band played on live TV on January 4 on *Happening for Lulu*, hosted by pop singer Lulu (whose best-known song was "To Sir With Love"). They were supposed to play two songs, and then Hendrix was supposed to sing a duet with Lulu. "I'm not going to sing with Lulu," he told Etchingham. "I'd look ridiculous."

Instead, a couple of minutes into the second song "Hey Joe," Hendrix stopped, announced the band was going to play a tribute to Eric Clapton, Ginger Baker, and Jack Bruce (the members of Cream, which had just broken up) and led the Experience in a long version of "Sunshine of Your Love" that took up the rest of the available time. The director kept signaling Hendrix to stop; off-camera, he gestured at the director with his middle finger and kept playing. The producer threatened Hendrix with never appearing on the BBC again.[23]

Lulu's reaction? "It was fab! Absolutely fab!"[24]

In interviews, Hendrix began to call his music "'Electric Church Music,' because it's like a religion to us." Sometimes he referred to it as "Sky Music."

"No Longer Playing as a Unit"

In mid-January the Experience started another tour of Europe. Chas Chandler attended the first concert, in Göteborg, Sweden, and called it "dire."[25] He thought the band was no longer playing as a unit.

The band next had two shows in Stockholm. Hendrix dedicated the first one to Eva Sundquist, a groupie he had met on a previous tour, calling her "a goddess from Asgard."[26] This was just a week after he had unveiled Kathy Etchingham as his girlfriend, but that night, Eva Sundquist became pregnant with Hendrix's son.

The Stockholm critics shared Chandler's opinion of the show in Göteborg. "Hendrix was listless and tired," wrote Ludvig Rasmusson. "He seemed like he had a desire to run away from it all. The joy of playing was gone." He called Redding and Mitchell "unimaginative musicians" and wondered why Hendrix had put up with them for so long. Redding would later say that show was particularly bad because he had trouble finding drugs in Sweden. Between shows he managed to get hold of a methamphetamine pill, which the band members divided amongst themselves.[27]

A few days later, in Düsseldorf, Germany, Hendrix met a tall blond ice-skating instructor named Monika Dannemann and talked with her all afternoon. (She later claimed he spent several days with her.)[28] Less than two years later, she would be the last person to see Jimi Hendrix alive.

Two concerts at the Royal Albert Hall in London, on February 18 and 24, followed the European tour. The first went badly. Hendrix had too much cocaine before going on. "He was so stoned, he was legless," remembered Trixie Sullivan. "I had to push him onstage." The second show was much better, ending with rare encores and a near-riot as fans tried to climb on stage.

Hendrix would not perform again in Britain for eighteen months.

"A Different Person"

In March, the Experience headed to New York to record for a month before starting yet another U.S. tour. For the first time, Hendrix asked Kathy Etchingham to join him. She arrived a week after the band. In the meantime, there was Devon Wilson, who told everyone she was Hendrix's girlfriend. Wilson was into cocaine and heroin, and Hendrix began copying her and relying on her to obtain drugs for him.

Wilson vanished before Etchingham arrived. Etchingham had never been with Hendrix in New York before, and she found it unsettling. Hendrix seemed like a different person, "trailing an enormous entourage like the colorful leader of some circus freak show. . . . There never seemed to be less than twenty people." The women, she said, looked like prostitutes, while "the men all appeared to be pimps and drug dealers, with their cool shades and little spoons hanging round their necks." But when she asked Hendrix who they were, he just called them "my friends."[29]

To journalist Sharon Lawrence, though, he provided a list of these "friends": "Producers. Would-be producers. Musicians. Guys that want to be musicians or work for the band. Girls that want to be singers. Dope addicts. Drug dealers. About a hundred million chicks that like to be around the scene. Designers. Models. A lot of guys who want or need money. A few thieves."[30]

When Etchingham discovered one of the drug-dealers among Hendrix's "friends" came complete with a .45-caliber revolver, she decided she did not like being in New York with Hendrix and returned to England, effectively ending their relationship.

She finally realized, she said, "there were no long-term prospects with Jimi. There was no way I was going to tame him. I wanted a decent family." She thought that, sadly, Hendrix wanted a family as well. "He just didn't know how to get it."[31]

Over ten weeks, the Experience played twenty-nine shows in the United States, before 350,000 people, earning $1.3 million (equivalent to more than $7 million today).[32] Violence marred many shows. Advocates of "Black Power," a militant civil-rights movement that emphasized self-determination by African Americans over integration, criticized Hendrix for using white musicians and having a white promoter. They accused him of selling out to white people, even though, as promoter Pat O'Day reminded him, the white people worked for him, not the other way around.

More than once, the Black Panthers came calling, backstage or wherever Hendrix was staying. One even approached Kathy Etchingham in London while Hendrix was on tour in America.

On April 29 in Oakland, Hendrix received an after-concert note from Diana Carpenter, who as a young prostitute had been his girlfriend in New York while he was a struggling musician. He sent word to her to follow his limousine to the airport, and they met in the terminal for the first time in three years.

Carpenter handed Hendrix a photograph of a child she claimed was his daughter. "This is Tamika," she said. "She's two years old."

"She has my eyes," Hendrix responded. He talked to Carpenter for another hour, mostly complaining about

Jimi Hendrix and the Black Panthers

The Black Panthers were formed in 1967 by black activists who rejected Dr. Martin Luther King Jr.'s pacifist approach to the struggle for equal civil rights. Instead, they called for a violent revolution to seize those rights.

Hendrix always made it clear that he was not interested in becoming involved in black politics—he preferred to let his music do his talking for him—and that he supported King's non-violent approach, but the Panthers kept coming after him, trying to pressure him into giving them money.[33]

Reporters kept asking Hendrix what he thought of the Panthers. The closest he ever came to expressing support was to say, "I naturally feel a part of what they're doing, in certain respects, you know. But everybody has their own way of saying things. They get justified as they justify others, you know; in their attempts to get personal freedom. That's all it is." He said he was with them "but not the aggression or violence or whatever you want to call it. I'm not for guerrilla warfare."[34]

Vague answers like that kept everyone guessing what his true beliefs were. Even those closest to him were not sure. Like a chameleon, he seemed to change beliefs to suit the situation.

how tired he was of touring. He took the photograph with him when he left.[35]

Busted

On May 3, the band flew into Toronto. As Hendrix went through customs at 9:30 A.M., Royal Canadian Mounted Police officers searched his bags. Along with the picture of Tamika Carpenter and a few other things, they found a small glass vial containing six packages of white powder and a small dark residue of resin. At 1:30 P.M. Hendrix was arrested for possession of heroin and hashish.

The drug bust did not get much publicity at first beyond the local newspapers. Michael Goldstein, Hendrix's public relations manager, bribed an Associated Press editor with a case of liquor to keep the news off the wire service. It would be a month, and the tour would be nearly over, before *Rolling Stone* would carry a piece on the arrest, strongly implying Hendrix had been framed.[36]

Hendrix denied the drugs were his. The fact that Mounties, rather than customs officers, did the search indicated the police had been tipped of. Hendrix argued in court that someone else had slipped the drugs into his bag. Privately he said he thought a disgruntled groupie must have planted them, then tipped off the police.

Hendrix's public statement painted the arrest as an attack by the Establishment on youth culture. "All of that is the Establishment fighting back," he said. "Eventually they will swallow themselves up. But I don't want them to swallow too many kids up as they go along."[37]

The police let Hendrix perform the night of the arrest, but escorted him to the concert. He paid $10,000 bail and continued the tour. His first court date was set for June 19. If convicted, he could face up to ten years in prison.

A sold-out show at Madison Square Garden shortly

Formed in 1966, The Jimi Hendrix Experience consisted of (left to right) Noel Redding, Jimi Hendrix, and John "Mitch" Mitchell.

after the Toronto performance drew 18,000 people and earned Hendrix $14,000 a minute. That made him the highest-paid rock star in the world—and the target for more criticism, for his high ticket prices ($5.50, about $30 today[38]). "The Hendrix concert grossed around $35,000 of YOUR bread!" wrote the *San Diego Sun*. "That's $19,000 to the performer. Okay, who is the villain here? That's right, kiddies, our HEROES are screwing us!"[39]

A Midnight Tour of Seattle

Three weeks after being arrested in Toronto, Hendrix had another show in Seattle, this time at the Coliseum.

92

Carmen Borrero accompanied him. Due to a downpour, people cleared out of his dressing room pretty quickly. Hendrix surprised a teenaged fan waiting for an autograph by asking him, "You got a car?"

The teenager led Hendrix and Borrero to a run-down, rusted-out Volkswagen Beetle. For the next two hours, at Hendrix's direction, the teenager drove Hendrix and Borrero to the places Hendrix had known growing up. One place they stopped was a hamburger stand where Hendrix had always wanted to take his girlfriend in junior high school, but had never had enough money for. As it turned out, the highest-paid rock star in history did not have any cash with him, so his impromptu chauffeur bought him a hamburger.

"On every block there was someplace he had stayed," said Borrero. "He had stories about every one." Hendrix even suggested driving to his mother's grave in Renton, south of Seattle, but that would have taken half an hour, and it was after 3:00 A.M. The teenager wanted to go home, Borrero was tired, and the band had to fly out in just a few hours for a show in San Diego that evening. So they called it a night.[40]

Shortly thereafter, in Los Angeles, Hendrix told *Rolling Stone* he would soon be touring with a different band. It was the first the members of the Experience had heard of it. But then, Hendrix told different reporters different things. He assured the *New Musical Express*, and the *Rolling Stone* reported to its readers on May 17, "the Experience has no intention of disbanding."[41]

At Hendrix's preliminary hearing in Toronto on June 19, he wore a suit for the first time in years. The trial was set for December 8. Hendrix flew black to Los Angeles for a June 22 performance at the Newport Pop Festival. The band received its largest paycheck yet, $100,000, but the show went so badly Hendrix swore at the audience and played much of the concert with his back to them.

> **"[The Establishment] will swallow themselves up."**
>
> **—Jimi Hendrix**

Redding blamed the court hearings. To make up for the poor performance, the next day Hendrix came back unannounced and jammed with Buddy Miles and Eric Burdon.

The End of the Experience

The next week in Denver, before a show at Mile High Stadium as part of the Denver Pop Festival, a journalist ran into Noel Redding. "What are you doing here? I thought you had left the band," he said. The question arose from Hendrix's public complaints to the press, but it turned out to be an omen. The Experience was about to play its last—and possibly worst—show ever.

Fans demanding free admission had rioted outside the stadium. Hendrix was in a bad mood, possibly due to drugs. He taunted the crowd, changing words in "Voodoo Child" to "Gonna make a lot of money and buy this town/Gonna buy this town and put it all in my shoe." Then he announced from the stage, to the complete shock of everyone involved with the band, that "this is the last gig we'll ever be playing together."[42]

Rioting broke out among the 17,000 people in the stadium. Some tried to climb onstage. Police fired tear gas into the crowd. When it drifted on stage, the band fled. With Herbie Worthington, they piled into the back of a U-Haul truck driven by road manager Gerry Stickells. He tried to escape through the crowd. Some fans had climbed on top of the truck to escape the tear gas, and their weight began to snap the roof supports. "They were pounding on the doors and the roof, and you could see the sides of the van start to buckle," Worthington remembered.[43]

Redding promised himself that if he survived, he would board a plane to England and never come back. True to his word, he flew home the next day. Hendrix flew to New York.

The Experience never played together as a trio again.[44]

Chapter 7

From Woodstock to the New Experience

Hendrix called his old army friend Billy Cox and asked if he would play bass. Cox and Mitchell began rehearsing in New York. Hendrix claimed losing Redding was not a huge setback, but over the next few months he only played one festival, one street fair, and two theatre concerts, a vast decrease from his previous schedule.

With Kathy Etchingham having gone back to London, Hendrix spent most of his time with Carmen Borrero or Devon Wilson. He also made friends with Colette Mimram and Stella Douglas, who owned a boutique where he liked to shop. They, along with the wealthy Deering Howe (his family owned several hotels), were Hendrix's first adult friends who were not part of the music business. "I think part of the attraction was that I came from money, and there was nothing I wanted from him," Howe said. "We had almost nothing in common except for a love of music."[1]

At their frequent dinners, they talked about art, philosophy, religion, and politics—anything but business. "We'd expose him to a certain refinement that he had never experienced before," said Mimram.[2]

Gypsy, Sun, and Rainbows

The pressure was on Hendrix to finish a new album. To try to speed that process, Jeffrey rented an eight-bedroom house (complete with riding stable, pool, cook, and housekeeper) in rural Shokan, New York, a few miles from Woodstock, where Jeffrey had his own country house. The rent was $3,000 a month—around $16,000 a month today.[3]

The cook, Claire Moriece, remembered Hendrix as a "sweet, humble, funny guy. . . . He felt like he was really lucky and he just expressed gratitude. . . . I baked blackberry pies and I made lots of different soups. Jimi loved soup and chocolate-chip cookies and corn cakes."[4]

Hendrix decided he would build the bigger band he had always wanted. He hired Larry Lee from Nashville for rhythm guitar, and Jerry Velez and Juma Sultan, whom he had met in New York clubs, for percussion. All three, along with Billy Cox, moved into the Shokan house and started trying to form a band—without a drummer. Mitch Mitchell was a question mark.

One day, Hendrix left for New York to say goodbye to Deering Howe, who was off to meet Colette Mimram and Stella Douglas in Morroco—and on the spur of the moment, decided to join him. Hendrix phoned Jeffrey (who was furious) and got the permission of the Royal

Canadian Mounted Police, who had to approve any travel outside the United States while Hendrix still faced drug charges. He did not tell the band: they did not know he was gone until they wondered why he had not returned from New York.

The trip to Morocco, Howe said, was "the best, and maybe the only, vacation [Hendrix] had. . . . It was amazing to watch him, as a black man, experience Africa. He loved the culture and the people, and he laughed more than I'd ever seen him laugh." For nine days Howe, Mimram, and Douglas toured North Africa.

"The vacation seemed to give him nourishment," Mimram said. "It recharged him."[5]

(Oddly, Hendrix later told friends he did not enjoy himself very much, because it was hot and because he thought he was being followed by men he did not know.)[6]

Back in the United States, Hendrix seemed revitalized . . . but also troubled by a premonition of death. A renowned Moroccan clairvoyant had done a Tarot card reading, and one of the cards she had pulled had been Death. In French, she told Mimram that the card did not mean Hendrix would die, that it could mean "rebirth," but before he heard the translation Hendrix cried, "I'm going to die!"

Over the next few months, he kept saying he was doomed. "Sometimes it would be 'I'm going to die in three months,' and sometimes it would be that he was only going to live for 'six months,'" Mimram said. "But he kept repeating that he was going to die before he was thirty."[7]

Hendrix's first concern, though, was to whip his new band into shape for an upcoming concert at a festival scheduled for Max Yasgur's farm, not far away near Bethel. The festival, though, took its name from the larger town of Woodstock.

Woodstock

Formally called "The Woodstock Music and Arts Fair," subtitled "An Aquarian Exposition," and promoted as "Three Days of Peace and Music," the festival was expected to attract 100,000 people at most; about 60,000 advance tickets were sold. Hendrix was the headline act, and the highest-paid performer there, contracted to receive $32,000—considerably less than he had earned at other shows. (That's equivalent to about $170,000 today.)[8]

Hendrix auditioned new drummers, but eventually brought Mitch Mitchell back. "The band was grim, a shambles," Mitchell wrote in his memoir, *The Hendrix Experience*, and it did not seem to get any better with practice. (Others in the band disagreed.)[9]

By the time the festival began, it was obvious organizers had seriously underestimated attendance. An estimated 800,000 people turned up. Another 200,000 tried, but gave up and went home. The two-hour drive from New York took ten hours that day, and traffic did not move at all for the last twenty miles, forcing people to hike a considerable distance.

"No one knew, no one suspected, no one had any

idea," said Billy Cox. "We thought it was just a gig where a lot of good musicians were going to be."[10]

There were only six hundred portable toilets on the site. Emergency food and medical staff were flown in by helicopter. Three people died, and two babies were born. But there was also music: Santana; the Grateful Dead; Janis Joplin; the Jefferson Airplane; Sly and the Family Stone; the Who; Crosby, Stills, Nash and Young—and, last on the bill, Jimi Hendrix, scheduled to play at 11:00 P.M. on Sunday. He was supposed to catch a helicopter at a local airport, but weather socked it in, so instead Hendrix's band joined forces with some other bands, including Crosby, Stills, Nash and Young, to steal a truck and drive to the site.

When they got there, they discovered the show was nine hours behind schedule. Hendrix's band waited in a nearby cottage all night, finally taking the stage at 8:30 A.M. on Monday morning. Only forty thousand people were still on hand. The band was introduced as the Jimi Hendrix Experience, but Hendrix corrected that. "We got tired of 'the Experience,' . . . so we decided to change the whole thing around and call it 'Gypsy, Sun, and Rainbows.'"[11]

The show was the longest Hendrix ever gave: sixteen songs over two hours. Many of the songs, woefully unrehearsed, were really just extended jams. More of the crowd left as the band played. "You can leave if you want to," Hendrix called after them. "We're just jamming, that's all. Okay? You can leave, or you can clap."

And then he played "The Star Spangled Banner."

"The sun came up directly in front of Jimi as he played," said Dave Myers, who was filming the festival. "He was playing for himself. Concentrating like I'd never seen anyone concentrate before. It was all in his fingers. His beautiful magic fingers."[12]

Hendrix's drawn-out, distorted version of the song, full of feedback, guitar-imitated explosions, and ambulance wails, had been part of his show for a year; he probably played it first on August 17, 1968, in Atlanta.[13] But at that time, in that place, wrote the pop critic for the *New York Times*, Al Aronowitz, "It was the most electrifying moment of Woodstock, and it was probably the single greatest moment of the sixties. You finally heard what that song was about, that you can love your country, but hate the government."

"Everything seemed to stop," remembered Roz Payne, who was working as a nurse on site. "Before that, if someone would have played 'The Star Spangled Banner,' we would have booed; after that, it became *our* song."[14]

To Hendrix, it was not a political statement. Later, he said, "We're all Americans . . . it was like 'Go America!' . . . We play it the way the air is in America today. The air is slightly static, see." Nor did he intend it as an anti-Vietnam War anthem. Earlier, he had dedicated another song to the soldiers in the Army.[15] Having been in the Army himself, and having friends serving in Vietnam, Hendrix always felt a connection to the armed forces. Earlier, he had made several

Jimi Hendrix on the stage at Woodstock on Monday morning, August 18, 1969.

statements defending the Vietnam War. "Of course, war is horrible, but at present it's still the only guarantee of peace," he said in 1967.[16]

But thanks to the Woodstock documentary film soon to play to millions more people than were actually there that morning at Yasgur's Farm, Jimi Hendrix's version of "The Star Spangled Banner" became an icon of the anti-establishment "youthquake" then shaking the country.

Hendrix's encore, after a couple of more songs, was "Hey Joe"—a song he had played in Café Wha? to tiny crowds of teenagers just three years before. When it was done, so was Woodstock.

Jimi Hendrix Hits Harlem

After Woodstock, the new band recorded a few tracks, including "Machine Gun." They also rehearsed for an upcoming free street fair in Harlem (which came about partly to defuse a move among Harlem mobsters to force Hendrix to play a concert).[17]

On the afternoon of the fair, Hendrix drove to the concert site in his Corvette Stingray with Mitchell, parked on the street, and had his guitar stolen out of the back seat before he had even gotten out of the car. His friends the Aleems were able to track down the thief and force him to return the instrument.

Hendrix had told the *New York Times* that "I want to show them that music is universal—that there is no white rock or black rock." But the concert started badly when Hendrix, in a strange echo of the incident in Louisiana the year before, was threatened by people in the crowd for being with a white woman, Carmen Borrero.

It was midnight when Hendrix reached the stage. Just like at Woodstock, many people had already left. Mitchell got booed just for being white; Hendrix got booed for wearing white pants. Someone threw a bottle against an amplifier; someone else threw eggs. By the time Hendrix actually started playing, only about five hundred people out of an initial five thousand were still on hand. By the time he finished, there were maybe two hundred. It was probably the toughest crowd he ever faced. Juma Sultan called the show "a draw."

Afterward, Hendrix found a parking ticket on his car.[18]

Five days later, a month after its first show, Gypsy, Sun, and Rainbows played its last show, a disastrous, sound–problem-plagued press showcase at a club called the Salvation that went on so late most of the journalists had left. Two weeks later, the band officially disbanded.

Hendrix on Trial

In the fall of 1969, Hendrix leased the only place of his own he would ever have in New York, an apartment at 59 West Twelfth Street in Greenwich Village. "The place looked like a Moroccan bazaar," Colette Mimram remembered. "You could imagine a hookah [a water-filled Middle Eastern pipe] sitting in the middle of the floor. There were African textiles all over the ceiling."

Hendrix celebrated his 27th birthday on November 27 by watching the Rolling Stones perform at Madison Square Garden, and afterward attended a party thrown by Devon Wilson for Hendrix and the Stones at an apartment belonging to a friend of hers. Ten days later, he flew to Toronto for his trial on charges of heroin and hashish possession.

No one could deny the drugs had been in Hendrix's luggage, so the defense was that Hendrix did not know they were there. He described all the things fans had given him over the years. When asked about his drug history, he fudged the truth—a lot. He said he had used cocaine "twice" and LSD "five times." He admitted he had smoked marijuana and hashish recently, but insisted he had never used heroin or amphetamines and claimed he was using fewer drugs than he had been. Finally, he said that on his last day in Los Angeles, he had had a headache, and a "girl with a yellow top" had given him a vial of what he thought was Bromo-Seltzer, which he had then stuck in his bag and forgotten about.

UPI reporter Sharon Lawrence also testified. She

The Case of the Missing Rock Star

One of the strangest incidents in Jimi Hendrix's life was the time he was kidnapped.

It happened not long after Gypsy, Sun, and Rainbows disbanded. Hendrix left the Salvation Club with someone he did not know, allegedly in search of cocaine. Instead of scoring drugs, he was held hostage in an apartment. The kidnappers contacted Michael Jeffrey and demanded Hendrix's contract as ransom.

Rather than pay, Jeffrey hired his own thugs to track down Hendrix's kidnappers. All they found was Hendrix, at the house in Shokan, unharmed.

According to Trixie Sullivan, Jeffrey talked to someone in the Mafia to negotiate Hendrix's release.

The entire incident went unreported in the press.

said she had been in the hotel room when Hendrix said he was feeling ill, and confirmed a fan had passed him something. Chandler was also called as a witness. He talked about all the gifts of drugs that had been given to members of his old band, the Animals.

The twelve-person jury deliberated for eight hours, and came back with a verdict of not guilty, "the best Christmas present I could have," Hendrix said. He flew back to New York and immediately got stoned on hashish.[19]

Where Is that Album?

The pressure on Hendrix for a new album intensified. Electric Lady Studios was behind schedule and over-budget. Worse, Ed Chalpin had finally settled the U.S. side of his legal battle for a piece of Hendrix's contract for a cut of all three of Hendrix's albums to date and the entire profits of his next album.

Hendrix therefore decided the next album would be of a live performance. He formed a new trio, Band of Gypsys, featuring Billy Cox and a drummer from his past, Buddy Miles. They rehearsed for ten days late in December in order to record four shows on New Year's Eve and New Year's Day at the Fillmore East.

Hendrix spent a picture-perfect Christmas with Carmen Borrero in Deering Howe's penthouse apartment at the top of the Hotel Navarro, drinking champagne out of crystal glasses and watching a light snow fall over Central Park.

A week later, Band of Gypsys played at Fillmore East.

Among those who attended was jazz superstar Miles Davis. (Hendrix and Davis admired each others' work and talked about recording together, but nothing ever came of it.)

The first show was mediocre. In fact, some people walked out. At the intermission, promoter Bill Graham needled Hendrix. "You're all jive tonight. Can't you do better than this?"[20]

Surprised and angry, Hendrix did so much better in the next show that Graham later told *Rolling Stone* he thought the Band of Gypsys played perhaps the best set he had ever heard in his hall.[21] It was, he said, "the most brilliant, emotional display of virtuoso electric guitar playing I have ever heard. I don't expect ever to hear such sustained brilliance in an hour and fifteen minutes. He just stood there, did nothing, just played and played and played."[22]

"He seems to be more concerned with creating an environment of intense sound and personal fury than he is with performing a particular composition," wrote the puzzled *New York Times* critic. "Jimi Hendrix playing a Jimi Hendrix song is one of the least-understandable performers to someone who is not a full-blown rock follower. He really is a piece of the underground scenery, and has to be appreciated as such."[23]

The Final U.S. Tour

The new band was short-lived. The Band of Gypsys' last performance came four weeks later at the "Winter Festival for Peace" benefit at Madison Square Garden.

Once again the show ran late. By 3:00 A.M. Hendrix was in bad shape. "When I saw him it gave me the chills," said blues guitarist and singer Johnny Winter, who was backstage. "It was the most horrible thing I'd ever seen . . . it was like he was already dead. . . . He really wanted to do that gig, but he never should have."[24]

Hendrix played one song and part of another, then abruptly quit and sat down in front of the amps. He had to be led offstage. Some people claimed Michael Jeffrey had given Hendrix too much LSD to wreck the show; but Hendrix himself claimed Devon Wilson had spiked his drink.[25]

Shortly after that, Buddy Miles headed back to Nashville. "*Mr.* Miles didn't hear the songs the way I did," Hendrix told journalist Sharon Lawrence.[26]

In February, Hendrix announced the original Experience would be reforming. Mitchell and Redding were brought to New York for publicity interviews, tickets went on sale—and then Hendrix changed his mind and replaced Redding with Billy Cox. He did not tell Redding, leaving that to his management.

The new band, sometimes billed as the Experience and sometimes as Cry of Love, started its U.S. tour on April 25 at the Forum in Los Angeles. For four concerts, one of the opening acts was Ballin' Jack, a group that included two Seattle musicians, Ronnie Hammon and Luther Rabb. Rabb had been in Hendrix's first band, the Velvetones. Hendrix's drug use worried Rabb. "He was over the line. He was aware that it was hurting him. He was making efforts, but somehow, through management or someone, people were always funneling drugs to him."[27]

Most of the songs were new ones, including "Machine Gun" and "Message to Love" from the *Band of Gypsys* live album released the day before the tour started. But what the crowd really wanted to hear were the old Experience hits. "He hated singing those hits," Rabb said, "but he felt he had to. He still had an 'act,' . . . and he felt he had to do things like play behind his back because that's why people came to see him."[28]

On May 30, the band arrived in uneasy Berkeley, California, for two shows. Protests and riots at the University of California had led to a number of injuries and one death.

> "[Hendrix] was aware that [his drug use] was hurting him."
>
> —Luther Rabb

At the nearby Altamont racetrack, the Hell's Angels, hired to provide security, had killed a black man during a Rolling Stones concert. The incident led Hendrix to say he felt as if "the whole of America is going to pot" and got him thinking about moving back to London.

Hendrix's concerts had their own problems. Often protestors demanded free admission. In Berkeley, they tried to break in through the roof after being told they could not enter and threw rocks at those attending. Hendrix had been sick the previous week, even canceling a few shows, but however he felt, and despite the protests (which Hendrix did not see, since he entered through the stage door), he gave two of his best performances ever, captured on film by a crew Michael Jeffrey had hired.

Carlos Santana was in the audience. He said, "Very few people play fast and deep. Most play fast and shallow. But [John] Coltrane played fast and deep, so did Charlie Parker, and so did Jimi."[29] Coltrane and Parker were considered masters of jazz saxophone, so Santana's praise was high praise indeed.

Hendrix spent most of the spring and summer trying to complete a new album. He was not short of songs— he had enough for four albums—but he kept working and reworking the material. On July 1, for instance, he recorded nineteen takes of "Dolly Dagger" before deciding he had a master. Fortunately, recording costs were greatly reduced: by that time, Hendrix was recording in the Electric Lady studio he and Michael Jeffrey co-owned.

"He was very proud of that studio," said engineer Eddie Kramer. "Being a black man of his stature, making a lot of money, and owning your own studio in New York City, that was the pinnacle of success for him. He had suffered a lot of slings and arrows, but here he was on top."[30]

"He loved that studio, and he spent night after night there," said Deering Howe. "But he'd get hung up on a song, and one eight-bar thing would take three days."[31]

Nevertheless, by the beginning of summer Hendrix was beginning to get some idea of what he wanted on the new album. He never settled on a final title or a track list, though. For one thing, he wanted a triple album; Jeffrey wanted a single album.

The band flew out to concerts all over the country that summer. On July 4, they played the Atlanta Pop Festival in Byron, Georgia. It was, said a young fan, "Jimi at his best. He was classy and focused. It was beyond thrilling to hear Hendrix play 'The Star-Spangled Banner' on the Fourth of July."[32]

On July 17, the band played at Randalls Island in New York City for the New York Pop Festival. Radical groups demanded that the money from the concert be turned over or they would riot. Promoters made a donation to the groups to forestall that.

The concert did not go well. Hendrix did not go on until 4:00 A.M., and radio news broadcasts kept coming in over the sound system. The crowd booed when he dedicated "Voodoo Child" to Devon Wilson, Colette Mimram, Deering Howe, and a few others, and he swore at the audience. "These are my friends," he said. He swore at the crowd again as he ended the concert and said goodnight.[33]

It was not a very fitting farewell, but as it turned out, that was Hendrix's last performance in New York City.

A Last Visit Home

On July 27, Hendrix flew to Seattle for what would be his last visit. He played in Sick's Stadium, the old baseball stadium where, as a kid, he had watched Elvis Presley. He spent the afternoon at Al's house. He did not get to see Leon, who was in jail, but he met his eighteen-year-old sister Pamela for the first time since she was adopted out as an infant. She came by the house for an autograph; she got an autograph and a hug.

Several people commented later that Hendrix seemed exhausted. "Everyone thought it was drugs," said Dan Fiala, a promoter who had worked on several Experience shows, "but he was really beat; he was even beat-up looking. He had been working way too hard, going in the studio when he wasn't touring, and it was really getting him."[34]

Sometime that afternoon Hendrix called his high school girlfriend Betty Jean Morgan, whom he had once planned to marry. She was married but separated, living with her parents. She had not really followed his career, and they had lived very different lives. "It was a short conversation," she said.

The concert was almost cancelled because of a downpour: since the equipment was not grounded, the promoters were worried Hendrix would electrocute himself. He finally went on at 7:15 P.M. when the rain let up a little. He started the concert with his standard introduction, "I want you to forget about yesterday and tomorrow, and just make our own little world right here." But after someone threw a pillow on stage for an autograph (the same pillow had been autographed by Janis Joplin three weeks earlier), Hendrix became angry. He swore, kicked the pillow off the stage, and extended his middle finger to the crowd. Later he simply walked off stage for two minutes in the middle of a song, forcing Mitch Mitchell to cover with an improvised drum solo.

His final number was "Foxy Lady," and he left without an encore. He returned to his father's house to talk with friends and family. Then, about midnight, he went out with his cousin Dee Hall (Delores's daughter), Alice Harding (Dorothy's daughter), and Marsha Jinka (daughter of his new stepmother). He took some LSD, then had them drive him around Seattle to all the places he remembered. "He wanted to look at everything, every place," Alice Harding said. He even had them drive him down to Renton to visit his mother's grave, but in the dark they could not find the graveyard.[35]

Rainbow Bridge

From Seattle Hendrix flew to Hawaii to appear in a movie called *Rainbow Bridge*. Director Chuck Wein wanted to mix famous figures from yoga, art, music, and surfing and film what happened. *Rolling Stone* described the film, released in 1972, as "acid trip memorabilia." Charles R. Cross, in his biography of Hendrix, called it, "one of the oddest films ever made."[36] Hendrix biographers Harry Shapiro and Caesar Glebbeek said, "The best thing that can be said for *Rainbow Bridge* is that, after seventy-one minutes, it finishes."[37]

The best thing that happened to Hendrix in Hawaii was that he managed to wean himself off of heroin, which was not available on Maui (although marijuana, cocaine, and LSD were). When someone suggested they fly Devon Wilson in to bring drugs, Hendrix urged them not to; she would almost certainly have brought heroin. He told Melinda Merryweather, a member of the cast he became friends with, that he was trying to free himself from Wilson's grip. "Devon had that black widow thing going on, and it was like he was the nectar she sought," Merryweather said.[38]

Despite the chance to relax, Hendrix remained depressed. He still had money worries, and he still had legal problems: Diana Carpenter had brought a paternity suit against him, and her lawyers wanted a blood sample. (Hendrix never talked about Tamika in public as being his child, never tried to support her, and never met her. However, in an unreleased song called "Red Velvet Room," he sings about his child "Tami.")[39]

From Maui the band flew to Honolulu for their final show of the tour. Afterward, Mitch and Buddy flew home while Hendrix took a two-week vacation. He rented a small house and wrote music and poems. He wrote a long, rambling, emotional, and somewhat incoherent letter to his father, Al, ending with an apology for a fight they had on his last trip to Seattle.

Two days later, on August 14, he flew back to New York. "He didn't want to leave Hawaii," Wein said, "but there was a point where he had to go back to being Jimi Hendrix."[40]

Electric Lady Opens

Back he went into the studio. To his friends he seemed somewhat re-energized, but he also made it clear he did not think his career was going in the right direction. "All his audiences wanted to hear were the four big songs they knew, and Jimi wanted to play other stuff," Deering Howe said. "Artistically, it was like he was trapped back on the Chitlin' Circuit again, forced to play what someone else told him. He didn't feel he could break free of that."[41]

On August 26, the day before he was scheduled to fly back to England to prepare for a European tour, Hendrix attended the official opening of Electric Lady Studio. Guests included Yoko Ono, Mick Fleetwood, Noel Redding, and Johnny Winter. The party was a disaster: some of the guests were stoned, and they trashed the studio. Disgusted, Hendrix left early.[42]

Later he met up with Colette Mimram and Devon Wilson. Mimram had been thinking about going on the tour, but she had not been able to get a passport. Wilson wanted to go, but Hendrix did not want anything more to do with her. "Jimi really wanted to cut it off with Devon because of the drugs," Mimram said. "She was a junkie and he didn't want anything to do with that."

"I want you to leave," Hendrix told Wilson that night, and so she did.[43]

The next morning he flew to London. In three days he would play the massive Isle of Wight Festival, larger than Woodstock.

In three weeks, he would be dead.

Chapter 8

The Death of a Rock Star

In the three days between August 27, when he returned to London, and the Isle of Wight Festival, his first concert in the United Kingdom in a year and a half, Hendrix conducted more than two dozen interviews. He was full of plans for the future. "It's all turned full circle; I'm back right now where I started. I've given this ear of music everything. I still sound the same, my music's the same, and I can't think of anything new to add to it in its present state," he told Roy Hollingworth from *Melody Maker*. "Something new has got to come, and Jimi Hendrix will be there. I want a big band . . . full of competent musicians that I can conduct and write for. And with the music we will paint pictures of earth and space, so that the listener can be taken somewhere . . . I don't any longer dig the pop and politics crap. That's old fashioned. . . . When there are vast changes in the way the world goes, it's usually something like art and music that changes it. Music is going to change the world next time."

The final quote: "I'm happy, it's gonna be good."[1]

In London, Hendrix met Kirsten Nefer, a twenty-four-year-old Danish model, when she came by the Londonderry Hotel with Karen Davies, whom he knew from New York. They talked for hours, and she and Davies spent the night in the room next to Hendrix's bedroom. Nefer left at 10:00 A.M., but Hendrix showed up at her place an hour later and took her to lunch. He asked her to go to the Isle of Wight Festival with him the next day and she agreed.

Just as at Woodstock, the crowd at the Isle of Wight Festival had exceeded anyone's prediction. Around 600,000 people had turned up. It was chaos, and (also as at Woodstock) the show was running hours late.

Richie Havens saw Hendrix there and was shocked by how ill he looked. "He looked like he had been up for days," Havens said.[2]

Protesters were trying to tear down the fences, demanding the concert be free. Nefer and Hendrix, waiting in a trailer, could hear the noise. "It was horrible," Nefer remembered. "It was not the loving and beautiful thing they had planned."

Hendrix did not go on until 2:00 A.M. His guitar kept going out of tune. The sound system kept picking up walkie-talkie transmissions. Hendrix, who had split the crotch of his new costume earlier (Noel Redding's mother had helped mend it), thought his pants had split again and hid behind the amps to inspect them.

"Jimi looked weak to me," French photographer Jean-Pierre Leloir recalled. "He was thin, almost losing his pants. The sound from the loudspeakers was bad. I could see his unhappiness. He was not the strong guy I had seen before. Jimi did not have the same presence."[3]

As Hendrix played his last song, "In from the Storm," protestors launched flares onto the wooden awning protecting the stage, thirty feet over Hendrix's head. Security guards, anxious to keep the flames from spreading, charged onto the stage. Someone spread the rumor that Hendrix himself had set fire to the stage so he would not have to play an encore. "The show just fell apart at the end," remembered Nefer.[4]

Trouble in Scandinavia

Less than sixteen hours later, Hendrix was on stage again in Stockholm. He started late and played late—so late that the concert ended with an announcer telling the crowd that the show was over, because the amusement park next door, closed for the concert, needed to re-open.

Eva Sundquist was backstage. She had written Hendrix several times about their baby, James Daniel Sundquist. Hendrix had never responded. Eva asked Hendrix if he wanted to come to her home to meet the baby, but he was pulled away from her by the press of people without ever giving her an answer.

The tour went from bad to worse. At the next stop,

somebody secretly slipped a psychedelic drug to Billy Cox, probably in a drink. He reacted badly, alternating between paranoid raving, from which only Hendrix was able to calm him, and catatonia, where he would not move at all.

Kirsten Nefer flew in from London to Århus, Denmark, only to discover Hendrix had taken a handful of sleeping pills—he had been suffering from a cold and had not been able to sleep for three days—and was in bad shape. She recalled, "He was talking about spaceships in the sky. He was staggering. There was no sense to what he was saying." He insisted she sit next to him and hold his hand as he attempted to conduct interviews. That night, when they took a cab to the concert, he was stumbling and confused. He made it on stage, but played only two songs, totalling about eight minutes, before he dropped his guitar and collapsed. The concert was cancelled and all the ticket money refunded.

> "He [Hendrix] was not the strong guy I had seen before."
>
> —Jean-Pierre Leloir

Nevertheless, Hendrix tried to give an interview to a journalist when he got back to the hotel. He told Anne Bjørndal, "I'm not sure I will live to be twenty-eight years old. I mean, the moment I feel I have nothing more to give musically, I will not be around on this planet anymore, unless I have a wife and children; otherwise, I've got nothing to live for."[5]

He was "exhausted and scared," Bjørndal said.

"I mean that's how he appeared to me, scared, like a frightened child."[6]

Hendrix finally fell asleep at 6:00 A.M. When he woke at noon, he seemed better, though exhausted. Nefer, who had sat up talking with him all night (at one point he had claimed to be afraid of being alone with her, but at another point he had asked her to marry him), accompanied him to Copenhagen. There, she suggested he stay at her mother's house, since there was construction going on near his hotel. Nefer's mother made Hendrix soup, and he then slept for several hours. Later he sat down for spaghetti with Nefer, her mother, and several brothers and sisters, but reporters showed up at the house and interrupted the meal. Hendrix invited them in to meet his "new love."

He serenaded Nefer in his dressing room that night before the show, even though it made him late on stage—and despite the disaster the night before, played "the concert of the year," as one paper called it. Mitchell asked Nefer, "What have you done to him? Jimi hasn't played this good in years."

Hendrix spent the night at Nefer's mother's house. He asked Nefer to come with him to the next few shows in Germany, but after she had arranged for time off from the movie she was filming, told her he did not want her to come after all. "A woman's place is in the home," he said. Then he changed his mind again, but Nefer went back to her film, though she saw him off at the airport.

In Berlin the next day, Hendrix was in bad shape

again, and played poorly. His concert at a festival in Fehrman, scheduled for September 5, was postponed until September 6 due to bad weather. Like so many festivals, it was violence-plagued. When some audience members booed him when he finally made it on stage, he told them he did not care.

Moments after Hendrix left the festival, some Hell's Angels, who had already broken into the box office and stolen most of the money, set fire to the stage. It burned to the ground.

Hendrix returned to London. Billy Cox was still in bad shape from whatever drug he had been slipped, and he was not improving. The rest of the tour seemed in doubt.

The Last Week

On September 8, Kirsten Nefer checked in with Hendrix in London. She and Hendrix took the still-messed-up Cox out for tandoori chicken, then handed him over to a roadie and went to a movie. Hendrix cheered up during the movie but quickly became depressed again. He told Nefer he wanted to take two years off.

Cox took a turn for the worse that night. A doctor could not find anything physically wrong with him; he suggested Cox be sent home to America. He was, and recovered. With Cox gone, and a concert coming up September 13 in Rotterdam, Hendrix needed a new bass player. He called a few people but eventually decided to simply cancel the rest of the European tour.

Thursday, September 10, Hendrix went to a party for

former Monkee Mike Nesmith at the Inn on the Park Hotel. The next day he did a long interview with journalist Keith Altham, who had inspired Hendrix's guitar-burning routine (which he grew to hate: "I'm so sick of burning my guitar," he told Kirsten Nefer.)[7]

On Sunday, September 12, Hendrix spent more time with Nefer. She overheard a long argument he had over the phone with Devon Wilson. Wilson had heard he was involved with a Danish model and planned to come to London to see him. Hendrix told Wilson to get off his back and hung up.

The next day, Hendrix yelled at Nefer, accusing her of sleeping with George Lazenby, cast opposite her in the movie she was working on. When she refused to quit the film, "He shook me until I had blue marks all over," she said. She left in anger.[8]

> **"I'm so sick of burning my guitar."**
> **—Jimi Hendrix**

Although she tried to contact him later, she never saw or spoke to him again.

Lots of people had trouble finding Hendrix that week. Michael Jeffrey looked for him; Hendrix had told Chas Chandler he wanted to fire Jeffrey and have Chandler represent him again. Hendrix's lawyer looked for him; Hendrix kept missing scheduled appointments. Diana Carpenter's lawyers also looked for him—they still wanted him to take a blood test to prove he was the father of Tamika.

Kathy Etchingham, his old London girlfriend (since married), was not looking for him, but bumped into him anyway at Kensington Market. He was with a blonde woman she did not recognize and he did not introduce. He asked Etchingham to look him up at the Cumberland Hotel.

Hendrix made a point of tracking down Linda Keith. She had championed him in New York and led Chas Chandler to him, but they were no longer friends. He found her at a club called the Speakeasy and gave her a new Stratocaster guitar to pay her back for the instrument she had once helped him get in New York. When she opened the case later, she found that it also contained all the letters she had written him during the summer of 1966.

When Keith saw Hendrix, he was with the same blonde woman Etchingham had seen him with: Monika Dannemann, the German ice-skater Hendrix had met in Düsseldorf in 1969. She had tracked him down at his hotel sometime after Nefer stormed out. Dannemann later claimed she had maintained a close relationship with Hendrix since meeting him, but much of her story has been discredited. Nevertheless, she was with Hendrix for the last days of his life.

On the night of September 15, Hendrix and Dannemann showed up at Ronnie Scott's nightclub where Eric Burdon and War were playing. Hendrix, hoping to jam with his old friend, was not allowed backstage because he was obviously stoned. "For the first time I'd ever seen him, he didn't have his guitar," Burdon said. "When I saw him without that guitar, I knew he was in trouble."[9]

"His face was ashen, and his brown eyes appeared exhausted and even frightened. Never had I seen him like this," recalled journalist Sharon Lawrence, who was in the club that night. "This was beyond being merely high or out of it. Something very serious was going on inside Jimi. Something *terrible*. I didn't know what to say or what to do."[10]

Late the next day, Hendrix and Dannemann stopped by a party where Dannemann called herself "Jimi's fiancée." That night, they went back to Ronnie Scott's. This time, Hendrix got to jam.

The Final Day

Hendrix spent the night at Dannemann's hotel. On Thursday, September 17, he woke late. In the afternoon, he had tea in a garden outside Dannemann's room, where Dannemann photographed him. That afternoon, they went shopping. Hendrix also spent some time at his hotel; several people contacted him there by phone. Mitch Mitchell asked him if he wanted to come play with Sly Stone that night, but Hendrix failed to show up for the concert.

Sometime during the afternoon, Hendrix and Dannemann ran into Devon Wilson. Wilson invited Hendrix to a party. He said he would come.

As Hendrix and Dannemann drove toward his hotel, a man in a car rolled down his window and invited Hendrix to tea. Hendrix agreed, and they followed the car, which also contained two young women.

The young man was Phillip Harvey, a wealthy son

of an English lord. In his lavish home, with its Middle-Eastern décor, Hendrix, Dannemann, Harvey, and the women sat on pillows, smoked hash, drank tea and wine, and talked. Hendrix told Harvey he would be moving to London again.

Around 10:00 P.M., Dannemann, feeling left out of the conversation, left in a huff. Hendrix went outside; Harvey could hear them arguing. Worried that neighbors would call the police, Harvey went out and asked them to be quieter. At about 10:40 P.M., Hendrix came back in, apologized, and left.

Back at Dannemann's hotel, Hendrix took a bath, then sat down and wrote the lyrics to a song called "The Story of Life." An hour later, Dannemann took him to the party Devon Wilson had invited him to, at the home of Pete Kameron, co-founder of Track Records, which had released Hendrix's first single. Hendrix ate some Chinese food and took at least one amphetamine tablet, and likely several other drugs. Dannemann showed up after just half an hour and said she was there to pick up Hendrix. Told to come back later, she came back very soon. "[Hendrix] got angry because she wouldn't leave him alone," Angie Burdon (Eric Burdon's estranged wife) wrote later in a letter to Kathy Etchingham. "[Hendrix] asked Stella [Douglas] again to put her off, Stella was rude to her and the chick asked to speak to Jimi." Hendrix talked to Dannemann and left with her abruptly at around 3:00 A.M.[11]

It was Friday, September 18. Dannemann was the only

one with Hendrix for the next few hours. She said later she made him a tuna-fish sandwich before he went to bed, but according to Etchingham, Hendrix hated tuna, and no food was found in the apartment. Dannemann also said that at around 4:00 A.M., after Hendrix had drunk some wine, he asked for some sleeping pills. Since Hendrix often took sleeping pills to help him sleep, and since he had taken an amphetamine earlier, that seems believable.

Dannemann said she did not give Hendrix any sleeping pills but waited, hoping he would fall asleep naturally. At around 6:00 A.M., she said, he was still awake, but she took a sleeping pill herself and had a short nap.

Dannemann's German-made prescription sleeping pills, called Vesperax, were very powerful. The directions said to take only half a tablet at a time. One full pill should have put Dannemann into a deep sleep for hours, which makes her story of taking a pill at six and having a short nap suspect. "A more likely scenario," says Hendrix biographer Charles R. Cross, "is that earlier that morning, around four, she took a pill and slept through the next events."[12]

Some time while Dannemann was asleep, Hendrix found her sleeping pills. There were fifty; he took nine of them. He may have thought they were weaker than the American kind he was used to and simply took a handful of them.

Instead, they were much stronger. Nine pills were almost twenty times the recommended amount for a man of Hendrix's height and weight. He must have lost consciousness quickly. Sometime after that, the combination of alcohol and drugs in his system caused him to throw up in his sleep. He breathed in the wine and undigested food and was in such a deep, drug-induced sleep that his body did not cough it back out. Instead, he quit breathing.

A few minutes after that, he was dead.[13]

Panic and Horror

Dannemann must have panicked when she woke up. She began dialing Hendrix's friends. The first one she reached, still in the middle of the night (according to what Burdon told Sharon Lawrence) was Eric Burdon. She told him Hendrix was "sick, and couldn't wake up." Burdon urged her to call an ambulance right away but she did not. "She rang up again later," he told Lawrence. "She still hadn't done anything for him. . . . She said she had gone out for a packet of cigarettes. I screamed at her, 'Call the ambulance now!' It was too late."[14]

Dannemann did not call the ambulance until 11:18 A.M. Burdon got there at 11:27 A.M., well before the ambulance arrived, and realized that Hendrix was dead. Not wanting the ambulance attendants to find drugs in the apartment, for fear of the repercussions in the music community, he called a roadie to come help him clear out all the drugs and drug paraphernalia. He found the song Hendrix had written the night before, "The Story of Life." Based on the lyrics (it mentioned Jesus, life, and death), Burdon leaped to the assumption

Decades after his death, many of
the details regarding Hendrix's
passing remain unclear.

that Hendrix had committed suicide, a theory some people still believe.

"I made a false statement originally," Burdon said later. "I simply didn't understand what the situation was. I misread the note: I thought for sure it was a suicide note, so I felt that I should try and help cover that up, and get it over with me. Jimi had talked to me about suicide and death a lot, and I knew he was in a hole. I thought it was a goodbye note."[15]

Sharon Lawrence still thinks so. She finds the number of sleeping pills Hendrix took—nine—significant because of Hendrix's interest in numerology. She says he told her that nine was "his" number, the number that was "very good or very bad." She also believes the "song lyrics" were found beside the bed because Jimi *wanted* them to be found, since he normally placed finished lyrics in a burgundy leather portfolio. "There was nothing that Hendrix would have put on a record," she wrote. "They were the words—the musings—of a tired and troubled man. . . . For me, there could be no doubt of Jimi's intention, the choice he'd made. I thought back to several conversations about 'number-nine days' in the past year. It was absolutely meaningful to him. I was certain that he had *deliberately* confronted fate, made a conscious decision. If the Vesperax *pills—nine* of them— didn't do it, then he wasn't meant to die."[16]

By the time the ambulance arrived, everyone had left, leaving Hendrix's body unattended. "It was horrific," ambulance attendant Reg Jones said. "The door was

When Did He Die?

One story, first told by Monika Dannemann and still to be found in some biographies of Jimi Hendrix, is that Hendrix was alive when the ambulance arrived and choked to death in the back seat, where he had been propped up.

That story was (or should have been) put to rest for good in 1994 when Scotland Yard conducted an in-depth investigation and concluded that Jimi was almost certainly dead when the ambulance arrived, that the ambulance workers and doctors had done everything they could—and that much of Dannemann's story was either questionable or false.[17]

flung wide open, nobody about, just the body on the bed."[18] According to two physicians at St. Mary Abbott's Hospital, Hendrix was dead on arrival. He had been dead for several hours, but the official pronouncement was made at 12:45 P.M. The inquest found the cause of death to be "inhalation of vomit due to barbiturate intoxication." Vesperax, amphetamines, Seconal, and alcohol were detected in Hendrix's blood.

Hendrix's father Al received the news in a phone call from Henry Steingarten, Jimi's lawyer. "It was in the morning, and I was still in bed," Al said in his 1999 book *My Son Jimi*. "Oh, it hurt—it's still hard for me to talk about it."[19]

The Funeral

Hendrix's body, dressed in a flannel logger's shirt (the vomit-stained clothes he wore when he died were destroyed), was sent back to Seattle for burial. Since Hendrix had left no will, Al Hendrix became the executor and sole inheritor. Freddie Mae Gautier planned the funeral; Al was too grief-stricken.

The funeral was held on Thursday, October 1, at Dunlap Baptist Church in Seattle. Redding and Mitchell were both there, along with two hundred other people inside the church and another hundred or so outside, behind barricades. Many of Hendrix's family, friends, and acquaintances were there. Seattle mayor Wes Uhlman attended. So did jazz trumpeter Miles Davis (who said later he had not even attended his own mother's funeral).

A graveside service followed at Greenwood Memorial Cemetery in Renton. A musical wake was held at Seattle Center House. Redding and Mitchell briefly performed together, but Redding said, "You just couldn't think of having a jam without Jimi."[20]

"I believe in heaven," Al Hendrix wrote. "I don't know if it's the way they talk about it, that spirits are up there flying around with angels or something like that, but I do feel there's an afterlife where you'll see all your old friends and family members. I was raised that way, and Jimi was too. . . . I like to believe that's where Jimi is."[21]

The Aftermath

Legal wrangling over Hendrix's legacy quickly took over from grief. A "final settlement" with Michael Jeffrey fell apart when Jeffrey was killed in a plane crash on March 5, 1973. A lawyer named Leo Branton assumed control of Jimi's legacy, with Al's agreement. Branton had producer Alan Douglas take creative control of posthumous releases of Hendrix's recordings. By the mid-seventies, Branton and Douglas had complete control, paying Al $50,000 a year plus occasional additional sums.

During the 1980s, interest in Hendrix's music swelled as old recordings were re-issued in the new compact disc format and some of the hours of additional recordings that exist were released (though many are considered of inferior quality).

Al Hendrix began to wonder if Leon Branton was really the person he wanted running the estate and filed suit against Branton and Douglas in April of 1993, seeking to regain control. Seattle billionaire (and Jimi Hendrix fan) Paul Allen, one of the founders of Microsoft, who would later build the Seattle rock 'n' roll museum known as (what else?) the Experience, loaned Al $4.1 million to conduct the lawsuit.

In June of 1995 Branton and Douglas gave up future rights in exchange for $9 million. In July, Al created Experience Hendrix, LLC, and appointed his adopted stepdaughter, Janie Hendrix, to run it, and his nephew Bob Hendrix to help her.

Al died on April 17, 2002, of heart failure. He was eighty-two. The struggle over Jimi Hendrix's valuable legacy continued. Al's estate, mainly because it included copyright to Jimi's song catalog, was worth $80 million. His will split it among eleven relations, with the largest share, 48 percent, going to Janie.

Leon received only a gold record of Janie's choosing, even though he had been included in all of Al's wills prior to the last one, signed in 1998. A real estate developer, Craig Dieffenbach, put up several million dollars to enable Leon to sue Janie and Bob Hendrix in an effort to have the final will overturned in favor of the previous one. Seven relatives who were in the will joined the suit, because, they said, even though on paper they had trusts worth millions, Experience Hendrix was so poorly run by Janie Hendrix, and her salary of over $800,000 was so large, they might never receive anything.

At about the same time, Noel Redding sued Experience Hendrix, hoping to get a larger share of the money generated by the Experience records; but in May 2002, Redding died suddenly of liver disease. He was fifty-seven.

The trial concerning Al Hendrix's will began on June 28, 2004. At the last minute, Joe Hendrix, Leon and Jimi's little brother that Al had had adopted out, asked to be included in the estate. A blood test, however, revealed he was not Al Hendrix's son (which shocked everyone, because of the close physical resemblance), and so he was not allowed to be part of the suit.

On September 24, 2004, Judge Jeffrey Ramsdell upheld Al's will and denied Leon's claims. (In early 2005, Leon began an appeal.) However, Judge Ramsdell also ruled Janie Hendrix should be removed as trustee for the relatives' trusts and an independent party appointed.

Al was initially buried next to Jimi in Greenwood Memorial Park. Just before what would have been Jimi

Deaths in the Family

In the years since Hendrix's death, many of his friends and acquaintances have also died. Some died very shortly after he did: Janis Joplin died of a heroin overdose just three days after his funeral; she, too, was only twenty-seven. Devon Wilson died after falling through a window (under mysterious circumstances) at New York's Chelsea Hotel in February 1971.

Many other people whose lives intertwined with Hendrix's have died in the decades since. Miles Davis died in September of 1991. Angie Burdon, Eric Burdon's ex-wife, died in a knife fight in December of 1992. Chas Chandler died of heart trouble in July of 1996. Curtis Knight died of prostate cancer in 1999.[22]

Monika Dannemann committed suicide on April 5, 1996. After her stories about Hendrix's death were discredited by the Scotland Yard investigation in 1994, she wrote a book called *The Inner World of Jimi Hendrix* which repeated many of the same fables. Kathy Etchingham took her to court for defamation and won a court order barring Dannemann from making her assertions. When she continued to do so, Etchingham took her back to court. Dannemann was declared in contempt and ordered to pay all court costs. Two days later, she killed herself.[23]

Hendrix's 60th birthday, November 27, 2002, Jimi's and Al's remains were moved, at Janie Hendrix's instructions, to a new $1 million, thirty-foot-tall granite memorial a hundred yards north of the original site.

The grave of Jimi's mother, Lucille, is marked only by a brick bearing the name Mitchell, the name of her second husband, to whom she was married for only a month.[24]

Chapter 9

The Jimi Hendrix Legacy

The September 18, 2003, issue of *Rolling Stone* had as its theme "The 100 Greatest Guitarists of All Time." Topping the list: Jimi Hendrix. "He made the electric guitar beautiful," wrote Pete Townshend in a full-page tribute.[1]

"The story of electric guitar will forever be told in two parts: Before Jimi and After Jimi," is how Andy Ellis put Hendrix's legacy in perspective for *Guitar Player* magazine in September, 1995, twenty-five years after Hendrix's death.

There were many players before Hendrix who used the electric guitar within an established musical setting, Ellis wrote, "but when Jimi exploded on the scene with 'Purple Haze,' 'Manic Depression,' and 'Third Stone From the Sun,' in a flash we understood: Here was a *music* beyond anything ever heard before, conceived and born of electric guitar. . . . He was a disruptive force. . . .

He dressed and played and talked and lived differently from the rest. Jimi stretched our concept of sound, songwriting, and social behavior."[2]

That's Jimi Hendrix's legacy: he created something that had never been heard before and lived life in a way nobody had lived it before. He was, indeed, a rebel.

Unique Music

According to Hendrix biographers Harry Shapiro and Caesar Glebbeek, Hendrix took a "world view" of music (long before "world music" was a term anyone used), listening to and absorbing even-handedly everything from the classics to jazz to African and Asiatic rhythms and tunes. "Jimi never allowed himself to be hidebound by the limitations of rock 'n' roll, or constrained by the limitations of subjective preference, and always resisted any categorization of his music," they wrote.[3]

"Jimi Hendrix was, without doubt, the most innovative guitarist of his, or any other era," wrote John McDermott and Eddie Kramer in their book *Hendrix: Setting the Record Straight*. "While many have attempted to emulate his feats, none have been able to enlarge upon, or even match, his incredible achievements. His collected works, specifically his first five groundbreaking albums, stand among those by Robert Johnson, Charlie Parker, Miles Davis, Muddy Waters and Howlin' Wolf as consummate contributions to American music culture."[4]

"Jimi strapped on a guitar virtually every night of his adult life and he never repeated himself," wrote Shapiro and Glebbeek. He was "a revolutionary . . . many of the

effects that came out of a Hendrix recording session had
never been heard before. He was the first to harness
sound to electricity and the first to bring under control
all the technological accoutrements of guitar playing
(guitar, amps, fuzz-box, wah-wah
and so on) to sculpt a whole new
aural landscape."[5]

For that reason, in some ways
his influence on music is obvious.
Prince, for example, has repeatedly
acknowledged Hendrix's influence,
both as a musician and as a showman. Many heavy
metal guitarists owe an obvious debt to Hendrix's
use of feedback, the whammy bar, sustained harmonics,
and neck tapping: in a sense, Hendrix provided the
vocabulary heavy metal bands use to build their own
performances every night.

> **"He [Hendrix] made the electric guitar beautiful."**
> **—Pete Townshend**

"It had always been dangerous, it had always been
able to evoke anger," Townshend wrote in the 2003
Rolling Stone tribute. "If you go right back to the
beginning of it, John Lee Hooker shoving a microphone
into his guitar back in the 1940s, it made his guitar
sound angry, impetuous, and dangerous. The guitar
players who worked through the Fifties and with the
early rock artists . . . had a steely, flick-knife sound,
really kind of spiky compared to the beautiful sound of
the six-string acoustic being played in the background.
In those great early Elvis songs, you hear Elvis himself
playing guitar on songs like 'Hound Dog,' and then you
hear an electric guitar come in, and it's not a pleasant

sound. Early blues players, too—Muddy Waters, Buddy Guy, Albert King—they did it to hurt your ears. Jimi made it beautiful and made it OK to make it beautiful."[6]

But his influence reaches beyond the professional musicians who copy his techniques. "Jimi today is a genuine folk hero," said David Walsh, who, in 1996, helped form Little Kids Rock, an organization that provides free after-school musical education and musical instruments to elementary school students in several states. "The kids are exposed to a variety of artists and songs," said Walsh. "You might be surprised at how many children, even six- and seven-year-olds, are familiar with Jimi's style and some of his songs. They know Jimi equals guitar."[7]

More Than Just Magic Fingers

However, those who knew Hendrix best are anxious to tell people that Hendrix was more than just magic fingers. "What so many players today are missing is what Jimi had—feeling," said Jack Joseph Puig, a Los Angeles record producer. "A feeling is not transferable. It comes from the soul, which God makes innately unique to that one person. Without a doubt Hendrix is responsible for a whole approach to rock guitar and an attitude that, frankly, still hasn't been touched."[8]

"If people consider virtuosity as an electric guitarist was his sole contribution to rock 'n' roll, his memory is suffering an undeserved slight," wrote McDermott and Kramer, "for the manner in which he wed his talent and personality to also inspire his supporting cast, musically and professionally, and broke down barriers in the recording studio, on the concert stage, and also in the rich but hitherto uncharted world of rock 'n' roll business, was just as profound."[9]

"I feel sad for people who have to judge Jimi Hendrix on the basis of his recordings and film alone, because in the flesh he was so extraordinary," Townshend wrote. "He had a kind of alchemist's ability; when he was on the stage, he changed. He physically changed. He became incredibly graceful and beautiful."[10]

"His true legacy can never be summed up in the number of records and CDs sold or the dollar figures attached to his name," wrote Sharon Lawrence. "For Hendrix the great axis of the universe was music, and he reveled in its enlightenment, power, and pleasure, owning a gift that he was eager to share.

"That gift lives on."[11]

Chronology

1942—*November 27:* Johnny Allen Hendrix born at 10:15 A.M. at King County Hospital, Seattle, the son of Al and Lucille (née Jeter).

1945—*November:* Al Hendrix, after being discharged from the army on November 11, collects Johnny from Mrs. Champ in Berkeley, California; they return via train to Seattle.

1946—*September 11:* Johnny Allen Hendrix renamed James Marshall Hendrix.

1948—*September 8:* Starts kindergarten.

1950—*September 27:* Sister Cathy Ira Hendrix is born.

1951—*December 17:* Al and Lucille Hendrix divorce; Al gets custody of Jimmy and his brothers.

1955—*September:* Starts junior high school.

1957—*September 1:* Sees Elvis Presley perform at Sick's Stadium.

1958—*February 2:* Mother, Lucille, dies; gets a real guitar.

1959—*September 9:* Starts attending Garfield High School; Father buys him his first electric guitar; joins the Velvetones, plays first gig; joins the Rocking Kings, which later become the Tomcats.

1960—*October 31:* Drops out of Garfield High School.

1961—*May:* Is arrested for "taking a motor vehicle without permission"; three days later he is arrested again. His sentence is suspended, provided he joins the army; *May 31:* Enlists in the army for three years; *October 31:* Is ordered to 101st Airborne Division, Fort Campbell,

Kentucky; *November:* Meets Billy Cox at Fort Campbell. Soon after they form the King Kasuals.

1962—*July 2:* Is discharged from the army; *Winter:* Moves to Vancouver to live with his grandmother Nora; joins Bobbie Taylor and The Vancouvers.

1963—*March:* Works his way back to Tennessee, playing with "Gorgeous" George Odell and many others.

1964—*Early:* Arrives in New York City; wins first place in the Wednesday-night Amateur Contest at the Apollo Theatre; *March:* Joins the Isley Brothers and records and tours with them; *November:* Quits the Isley Brothers in Nashville; tours with Sam Cooke for a short time.

1965—*January:* Meets Little Richard in Atlanta and becomes guitar player with the Upsetters, Little Richard's band; *February:* In Hollywood, starts calling himself Maurice James; *July 27:* Signs a two-year contract with Sue Records; *October:* Joins Curtis Knight and The Squires; *October 15:* Signs a three-year contract with Ed Chalpin for PPX Inc.

1966—*January:* Joins the King Curtis band; *June/July:* Forms his own band, Jimmy James and the Blue Flames; *July 5:* Chas Chandler, at Linda Keith's urging, sees Jimmy James and the Blue Flames perform at Café Wha?; *September 9:* Chandler works out details with Hendrix to take him to England (changes his name from "Jimmy" to "Jimi" about now); *September 24:* Arrives in England; *September 29:* Meets Noel Redding and hires him as bass player; *October 1:* Jams with Cream, impresses Eric Clapton; *October 6:*

Mitch Mitchell hired as the drummer for the Jimi Hendrix Experience; *October 13:* The Jimi Hendrix Experience plays its first gig in Evreux, France; *October 23:* The Experience record "Hey Joe"; *November 2:* Recording begins on the first Experience album; *December 13:* TV debut on *Ready, Steady, Go!*; *December 16:* First single, "Hey Joe" (flip side, "Stone Free"), released in the United Kingdom.

1967—*February 3:* The Experience begins work on second single, "Purple Haze," and its follow-up, "The Wind Cries Mary."; *March 31:* Start of first U.K. tour, supporting The Walker Brothers; *April 4:* Last day of recording for the Experience's debut album, *Are You Experienced*; *May 4:* First day of recording for the second album; *June 18:* First American concert, at the Monterey Pop Festival in California; *July 8:* The Jimi Hendrix Experience begins its first U.S. tour, opening for The Monkees; *July 16:* The Experience drops out of The Monkees' tour; *July 30:* Jams with Curtis Knight at PPX Studios: Ed Chalpin will later release the recordings, prompting lawsuits; *October 30:* Work is completed on *Axis: Bold As Love*, the second Experience album.

1968—*January 4:* Arrested in Göteborg, Sweden, for trashing his hotel room; *April 18:* Serious work begins at the Record Plant in New York on the Experience's third album, eventually known as *Electric Ladyland*; *August 27:* Recording of *Electric Ladyland* concludes;

1969—*January 4:* Jimi commemorates the break-up of Cream by performing a seemingly unplanned rendition of "Sunshine of Your Love" on *The Lulu Show*, a live TV program; *May 3:* Arrested for drug possession at Toronto International Airport; *June 9:* The Experience plays its final show at the Denver Pop Festival; *August 14:* Begins rehearsals with a new band; *August 18:* The new band, Gypsy, Sun, and Rainbows, headlines the Woodstock festival; performance of "The Star-Spangled Banner" becomes an iconic moment of the 1960s; *August 28:* Resumes work on a new studio album; *November 7:* Forms The Band of Gypsys; *December 10:* Is found not guilty in Toronto; *December 31:* Begins two nights of shows at the Fillmore East in New York, which become the Band of Gypsys live album.

1970—*January 28:* Leaves the stage just two songs into a New York performance; the Band of Gypsys is disbanded soon afterwards; *February 4:* Reformation of The Jimi Hendrix Experience is announced; it never happens; *March 23:* Playing with Mitch Mitchell and Billy Cox, starts a series of sessions intended for a new album, tentatively titled *The First Rays of the New Rising Sun*; *May 30:* The trio, sometimes billed as the Experience, sometimes as Cry of Love, is taped and filmed during its performance at the Berkeley Community Theater in California; *June 15:* Begins using his new Electric Lady Studios in New York; *July 30:* Two shows on Maui are filmed for a movie called *Rainbow Bridge*; *August 1:* Performs his last U.S. concert; *August 22:* Final recording session at Electric Lady Studios; *August 27:* Flies to England; *August 30:* Performs at the Isle of Wight Festival;

September 6: Final full live performance in
Fehrman, West Germany; flies to London;
September 10: Last interview, with journalist
Keith Altham; *September 16–17:* Last public
appearance, jamming with Eric Burdon and War
at Ronnie Scott's in London; *September 18:* Dies
in the Samarkand Hotel in London; *October 1:*
Is buried in Greenwood Cemetery, Renton,
Washington.

Chapter Notes

Chapter 1. Guitar God

1. Charles R. Cross, *Room Full of Mirrors: A Biography of Jimi Hendrix* (New York: Hyperion, 2005), pp. 154–155.
2. Chris Potash, ed., *The Jimi Hendrix Companion: Three Decades of Commentary* (New York: Schirmer Books, 1996), pp. xv, xviii.
3. Cross, p. 156.
4. Ibid.
5. Ibid, pp. 176–177.
6. Sharon Lawrence, *Jimi Hendrix: the Man, the Magic, the Truth* (New York: HarperEntertainment, 2005), p. 217.
7. Ibid., p. 322.

Chapter 2. Early Days

1. Harry Shapiro and Caesar Glebbeek, *Jimi Hendrix: Electric Gypsy* (New York: St. Martin's Griffin, 1990, 1995), p. 13.
2. Charles R. Cross, *Room Full of Mirrors: A Biography of Jimi Hendrix* (New York: Hyperion, 2005), pp. 12–15.
3. Shapiro and Glebbeek, pp. 6–10.
4. Cross, p. 9.
5. Ibid, pp. 19–20.
6. Shapiro and Glebbeek, p. 13.
7. Cross, pp. 20–22.
8. Shapiro and Glebbeek, p. 13.
9. Cross, pp. 23–25.
10. Sharon Lawrence, *Jimi Hendrix: the Man, the Magic, the Truth* (New York: HarperEntertainment, 2005), p. 6.
11. Shapiro and Glebbeek, p. 18.
12. Lawrence, pp. 6–7.
13. Cross, p. 28.
14. Ibid., p. 30.
15. Lawrence, p. 10.

16. Cross, pp. 32–36.
17. Ibid., p. 39.
18. Ibid., p. 37.
19. Lawrence, pp. 11–12.
20. Cross, p. 37.
21. Lawrence, p. 13.
22. Shapiro and Glebbeek, pp. 23–24.
23. Lawrence, p. 14.
24. Cross, p. 46.
25. Ibid., p. 49.
26. Ibid., pp. 41–42.
27. Shapiro and Glebbeek, p. 25.
28. Cross, p. 43.
29. Shapiro and Glebbeek, p. 29.
30. Cross, p. 53.
31. Lawrence, p. 14.
32. Cross, p. 55.
33. Shapiro and Glebbeek, p. 38.
34. Ibid., p. 31.
35. Cross, pp. 58–59.
36. Cross, p. 59.
37. Lawrence, p. 15.
38. Ibid., pp. 62–65.

Chapter 3. The Music Begins

1. Charles R. Cross, *Room Full of Mirrors: A Biography of Jimi Hendrix* (New York: Hyperion, 2005), p. 66.
2. Sharon Lawrence, *Jimi Hendrix: the Man, the Magic, the Truth* (New York: HarperEntertainment, 2005), p. 17.
3. Harry Shapiro and Caesar Glebbeek, *Jimi Hendrix: Electric Gypsy* (New York: St. Martin's Griffin, 1990, 1995), p. 46.
4. Cross, p. 67.
5. Ibid., p. 70.
6. Ibid., p. 68.
7. Ibid., p. 69.
8. Ibid.
9. Ibid., p. 70.

10. Shapiro and Glebbeek, pp. 42–43.
11. Ibid., p. 72.
12. Ibid., p. 73.
13. Ibid., p. 79.
14. Shapiro and Glebbeek, p. 46.
15. Lawrence, p. 19.
16. Cross, p. 83.
17. Ibid., pp. 84–88.
18. Shapiro and Glebbeek, p. 60.
19. Lawrence, p. 24.
20. Shapiro and Glebbeek, p. 61.
21. Cross, p. 94.
22. Ibid., p. 95.
23. Shapiro and Glebbeek, p. 61.
24. Ibid., pp. 96–97.
25. Ibid., pp. 97–99.
26. Ibid., p. 101.
27. Lawrence, p. 28.
28. Shapiro and Glebbeek, p. 67.
29. Cross, p. 105.
30. Ibid., p. 111.
31. Ibid.
32. Ibid., p. 112.
33. Ibid., p. 115.
34. Shapiro and Glebbeek, p. 88.
35. Cross, pp. 120–121.
36. Ibid., p. 125.
37. Ibid., pp. 125–127.
38. Ibid., pp. 131–132.
39. Ibid., p. 132.
40. Lawrence, p. 35.
41. Cross, p. 140.

Chapter 4.   From Greenwich Village to Greenwich, England

1. Harry Shapiro and Caesar Glebbeek, *Jimi Hendrix: Electric Gypsy* (New York: St. Martin's Griffin, 1990, 1995), p. 104.

2. Sharon Lawrence, *Jimi Hendrix: the Man, the Magic, the Truth* (New York: HarperEntertainment, 2005), p. 41.
3. Ibid., pp. 146–147.
4. Ibid., p. 147.
5. Ibid., pp. 150–151.
6. Lawrence, p. 42.
7. Shapiro and Glebbeek, p. 108.
8. Lawrence, p. 48.
9. Cross, pp. 151–152.
10. Lawrence, p. 49.
11. Shapiro and Glebbeek, p. 110.
12. Ibid., pp. 159–160.
13. Ibid., pp. 117–118.
14. Lawrence, p. 53.
15. Cross, p. 162.
16. Shapiro and Glebbeek, p. 117.
17. Cross, p. 164.
18. Ibid., p. 165.
19. Lawrence, p. 53.
20. Cross, p. 165.
21. Lawrence, p. 60.
22. Cross, p. 166.
23. Ibid., p. 171.
24. Ibid., pp. 172–173.
25. Lawrence, p. 57.
26. Shapiro and Glebbeek, p. 126.
27. Cross, p. 174.
28. Ibid., p. 176.
29. Shapiro and Glebbeek, p. 146.
30. John McDermott, with Eddie Kramer, *Hendrix: Setting the Record Straight* (New York: Warner Books, 1992), p. 28.
31. Ibid., p. 30.
32. Cross., p. 180.
33. Ibid., p. 183.
34. Ibid., p. 181.
35. Ibid., p. 182.
36. Shapiro and Glebbeek, pp. 168–169.

37. *The Inflation Calculator*, n.d., <http://www.westegg.com/ inflation/infl.cgi> (September 2, 2005).
38. Chris Potash, ed., *The Jimi Hendrix Companion: Three Decades of Commentary* (New York: Schirmer Books, 1996), p. 12.
39. Cross, p. 184.

Chapter 5. Back in the U.S.A.

1. Charles R. Cross, *Room Full of Mirrors: A Biography of Jimi Hendrix* (New York: Hyperion, 2005), p. 185.
2. Ibid., p. 186.
3. Ibid., pp. 186–187.
4. Ibid., p. 187.
5. Ibid., p. 188.
6. Ibid., p. 189.
7. Sharon Lawrence, *Jimi Hendrix: the Man, the Magic, the Truth* (New York: HarperEntertainment, 2005), p. 76.
8. Cross, p. 190.
9. Ibid., p. 192.
10. Ibid.
11. "Owsley Stanley," Wikipedia, n.d., <http://en.wikipedia. org/wiki/Owsley_Stanley> (September 1, 2005).
12. Lawrence, p. 82.
13. Ibid., p. 193.
14. Harry Shapiro and Caesar Glebbeek, *Jimi Hendrix: Electric Gypsy* (New York: St. Martin's Griffin, 1990, 1995), p. 190.
15. Cross, p. 193.
16. Ibid., p. 193.
17. Lawrence, p. 78.
18. Cross, p. 194.
19. Ibid.
20. Ibid., pp. 194–195.
21. Lawrence, p. 79.
22. Cross, p. 196.
23. Shapiro and Glebbeek, p. 198.
24. Cross, p. 197.
25. Ibid.

26. Shapiro and Glebbeek, p. 419.
27. Lawrence, p. 85.
28. Cross, p. 198.
29. Lawrence, p. 85.
30. Cross, p. 202.
31. Lawrence, p. 86.
32. Shapiro and Glebbeek, p. 215.
33. Cross, p. 205.
34. Ibid., p. 207.
35. Ibid., p. 205.
36. Ibid., p. 207.
37. Shapiro and Glebbeek, p. 220.
38. Ibid., p. 235.
39. Cross, p. 208.
40. Shapiro and Glebbeek, p. 248.
41. Cross, p. 211.
42. Ibid., pp. 214–215.
43. Ibid., p. 215.
44. Ibid.
45. Ibid., p. 216.
46. Ibid., pp. 216–218.
47. Ibid., p. 221.
48. *The Inflation Calculator*, n.d., <http://www.westegg.com/inflation/infl.cgi> (September 2, 2005).
49. Cross, p. 223.
50. Shapiro and Glebbeek, p. 272.
51. Cross, p. 224.
52. Shapiro and Glebbeek, pp. 276–278.
53. Ibid., p. 292.

Chapter 6. Electric Ladyland

1. Sharon Lawrence, *Jimi Hendrix: the Man, the Magic, the Truth* (New York: HarperEntertainment, 2005), p. 100.
2. Harry Shapiro and Caesar Glebbeek, *Jimi Hendrix: Electric Gypsy* (New York: St. Martin's Griffin, 1990, 1995), p. 279.
3. Charles R. Cross, *Room Full of Mirrors: A Biography of Jimi Hendrix* (New York: Hyperion, 2005), p. 227.

4. Shapiro and Glebbeek, p. 281.
5. Ibid.
6. Ibid.
7. Lawrence, pp. 101–102.
8. Cross, p. 229.
9. Ibid.
10. Ibid., p. 231.
11. Ibid.
12. Ibid., p. 232.
13. Lawrence, p. 106.
14. Cross, pp. 236–237.
15. Ibid., p. 237.
16. Ibid., p. 238.
17. Ibid.
18. Ibid., p. 239.
19. Ibid., p. 241.
20. Lawrence, p. 105.
21. Cross, p. 242.
22. Ibid.
23. Ibid., pp. 242–243.
24. Lawrence, p. 120.
25. Shapiro and Glebbeek, p. 329.
26. Ibid.
27. Cross, pp. 243–245
28. Ibid., p. 245.
29. Ibid., p. 250.
30. Lawrence, p. 114.
31. Cross, pp. 250–251.
32. *The Inflation Calculator*, n.d., <http://www.westegg.com/inflation/infl.cgi> (September 2, 2005).
33. Shapiro and Glebbeek, pp. 368–369.
34. Chris Potash, ed., *The Jimi Hendrix Companion: Three Decades of Commentary* (New York: Schirmer Books, 1996), p. 28.
35. Cross, pp. 251–252.
36. Potash, pp. 18–21.
37. Cross, p. 254.
38. *The Inflation Calculator*.

39. Cross, p. 255.
40. Ibid., p. 257.
41. Potash, p. 22.
42. Shapiro and Glebbeek, p. 373.
43. Cross, p. 260.
44. Ibid., pp. 259–261.

Chapter 7. From Woodstock to the New Experience

1. Charles R. Cross, *Room Full of Mirrors: A Biography of Jimi Hendrix* (New York: Hyperion, 2005), p. 262.
2. Ibid.
3. *The Inflation Calculator*, n.d., <http://www.westegg.com/inflation/infl.cgi> (September 2, 2005).
4. Harry Shapiro and Caesar Glebbeek, *Jimi Hendrix: Electric Gypsy* (New York: St. Martin's Griffin, 1990, 1995), p. 380.
5. Cross, p. 264.
6. Shapiro and Glebbeek, p. 379.
7. Cross, pp. 265–266.
8. *The Inflation Calculator*.
9. Cross, p. 268.
10. Ibid.
11. Ibid., p. 270.
12. Sharon Lawrence, *Jimi Hendrix: the Man, the Magic, the Truth* (New York: HarperEntertainment, 2005), p. 158.
13. Shapiro and Glebbeek, p. 385.
14. Cross, p. 271.
15. Ibid., pp. 271–272.
16. Shapiro and Glebbeek, p. 387.
17. Cross, pp. 273–274.
18. Cross, pp. 275–276.
19. Ibid., pp. 280–282.
20. Lawrence, p. 175.
21. Chris Potash, ed., *The Jimi Hendrix Companion: Three Decades of Commentary* (New York: Schirmer Books, 1996), p. 27.
22. Shapiro and Glebbeek, p. 407.

23. Potash, p. 26.
24. Shapiro and Glebbeek, p. 413.
25. Cross, p. 290.
26. Lawrence, p. 176.
27. Cross, p. 291.
28. Ibid., p. 292.
29. Ibid., p. 296.
30. Ibid., p. 298.
31. Ibid.
32. Lawrence, p. 186.
33. Cross, p. 299.
34. Ibid., p. 300.
35. Ibid., pp. 303–305.
36. Ibid., p. 306.
37. Shapiro and Glebbeek, p. 432.
38. Cross, pp. 307–308.
39. Ibid., p. 308.
40. Ibid., p. 312.
41. Ibid., p. 313.
42. Shapiro and Glebbeek, pp. 442–443.
43. Cross, p. 314.

Chapter 8. **The Death of a Rock Star**

1. Chris Potash, ed., *The Jimi Hendrix Companion: Three Decades of Commentary* (New York: Schirmer Books, 1996), pp. 35–37.
2. Charles R. Cross, *Room Full of Mirrors: A Biography of Jimi Hendrix* (New York: Hyperion, 2005), p. 316.
3. Sharon Lawrence, *Jimi Hendrix: the Man, the Magic, the Truth* (New York: HarperEntertainment, 2005), p. 196.
4. Cross, pp. 317–318.
5. Ibid., p. 321.
6. Harry Shapiro and Caesar Glebbeek, *Jimi Hendrix: Electric Gypsy* (New York: St. Martin's Griffin, 1990, 1995), p. 454.
7. Cross, p. 322.
8. Ibid., p. 327.
9. Ibid., p. 329.

10. Lawrence, p. 202.
11. Cross, p. 331.
12. Ibid., p. 332.
13. Ibid., pp. 332–333.
14. Lawrence, p. 209.
15. Cross, p. 335.
16. Lawrence, p. 215.
17. Cross, p. 344.
18. Ibid., p. 336.
19. James Allen Hendrix, *My Son Jimi*, (Seattle: AlJas Enterprises, L.P., 1999), p. 171.
20. Cross, p. 340.
21. Hendrix, p. 174.
22. Cross, pp. 341, 343.
23. Cross, p. 344.
24. Cross, p. 352.

Chapter 9. The Jimi Hendrix Legacy

1. Sharon Lawrence, *Jimi Hendrix: the Man, the Magic, the Truth* (New York: HarperEntertainment, 2005), p. 323.
2. Chris Potash, ed., *The Jimi Hendrix Companion: Three Decades of Commentary* (New York: Schirmer Books, 1996), pp. 200–201.
3. Harry Shapiro and Caesar Glebbeek, *Jimi Hendrix: Electric Gypsy* (New York: St. Martin's Griffin, 1990, 1995), p. 499.
4. John McDermott, with Eddie Kramer, *Hendrix: Setting the Record Straight* (New York: Warner Books, 1992), p. 324.
5. Shapiro and Glebbeek, p. 502.
6. Pete Townshend, "Jimi Hendrix: The Greatest Guitarist of All Time," *Rolling Stone*, September 18, 2003.
7. Lawrence, p. 325.
8. Ibid., p. 322.
9. McDermott and Kramer, p. 324.
10. Townshend.
11. Ibid.

Selected Discography of Jimi Hendrix

Jimi Hendrix recorded three studio albums with the Experience and one live album with the Band of Gypsys. Since his death dozens of compilations of previously released and unreleased material have appeared—too many to list here.

The albums, with song lists, released during his lifetime were:

The Jimi Hendrix Experience:

Are You Experienced?
Purple Haze
Manic Depression
Hey Joe
Love or Confusion
May This Be Love
I Don't Live Today
The Wind Cries Mary
Fire
Third Stone from the Sun
Foxy Lady
Are You Experienced?

Axis: Bold as Love
EXP
Up from the Skies
Spanish Castle Magic
Little Wing
If Six Was Nine
One Rainy Wish

You've Got Me Floating
Castles Made of Sand
She's So Fine
Little Miss Lover
Bold as Love
Wait Until Tomorrow
Ain't No Telling

Electric Ladyland
. . . And the Gods Made Love
Have You Ever Been (to Electric Ladyland)
Crosstown Traffic
Voodoo Child
Little Miss Strange
Long Hot Summer Night
Come On (Part 1)
Gypsy Eyes
Burning of the Midnight Lamp
Rainy Days, Dream Away
1983 . . . (A Merman I Should Turn to Be)
Moon, Turn the Tides . . . gently gently away
Still Raining, Still Dreaming
House Burning Down
All Along the Watchtower
Voodoo Child (Slight Return)

Band of Gypsys:

Band of Gypsys
Who Knows
Machine Gun
Changes
Power to Love
Message of Love
We Gotta Live Together

Further Reading

Books

Cross, Charles R. Room *Full of Mirrors: A Biography of Jimi Hendrix*. New York: Hyperion, 2005.

Lawrence, Sharon. *Jimi Hendrix: the Man, the Magic, the Truth*. New York: HarperEntertainment, 2005.

Potash, Chris, ed. *The Jimi Hendrix Companion: Three Decades of Commentary*. New York: Schirmer Books, 1996.

Shapiro, Harry, and Caesar Glebbeek. *Jimi Hendrix: Electric Gypsy*. New York: St. Martin's Griffin, 1990, 1995.

Internet Addresses

A Jimi Hendrix Experience
http://www.musicfanclubs.org/jimihendrix

Jimi Hendrix Memorial
http://www.jimihendrixmemorial.com/

The Official Jimi Hendrix Website
http://www.jimi-hendrix.com/

Index